PROHIBITION PITTSBURGH

RICHARD GAZARIK

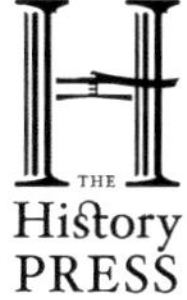

Published by The History Press
Charleston, SC
www.historypress.net

First published 2017

Manufactured in the United States

ISBN 9781467136624

Library of Congress Control Number: 2017940923

To Lucy, Katie, Adam and Kellie

Contents

Preface

Pittsburgh's reputation as a "shot-and-a-beer town" was derived from a concoction known as a "puddler's cocktail," a shot of whiskey and a glass of beer. The "boilermaker" was a variation of the drink, except that the shot glass of whiskey was dropped into the beer glass and allowed to settle to the bottom before drinking.

The boilermaker was a favorite drink of steelworkers, who headed for the nearest saloon when their shifts ended to wash away the day's grit in their mouths. Drinking in industrial Pittsburgh was something to be done quickly, like shaving. To make it convenient for customers, some saloons had urinals built into the bar so customers could urinate without interrupting their drinking.

Pittsburgh has always been a hard-drinking town even before the Whiskey Rebellion created an uproar in western Pennsylvania. After Prohibition was repealed, Pittsburgh residents became the "hardest drinkers" in the state. By 1937, city residents spent $15.5 million annually on liquor, more than Philadelphia.

The Pittsburgh area has undergone a transformation since the days when blue-collar workers bellied up to the bar ordering boilermakers. Craft breweries, wineries and distilleries have created a renaissance for alcohol in the Pittsburgh area. Pennsylvania's strict liquor laws have loosened a bit to allow the sale and tasting of alcohol on site.

Pittsburgh still is a hard-drinking town. *Forbes* magazine rated the city eleventh on a list of the fifteen hardest-drinking cities in the United States. Drinkers have become so sophisticated that bartenders are more likely to hear a patron order a glass of California Pinot Noir, a Steel City *aperitivo* or a Pittsburgh Sunrise than a shot and a beer.

Acknowledgements

I may never have had the chance to write this book if Karmen Cook hadn't rejected my proposal for another project and instead asked me if I'd be interested in writing a book about Prohibition in Pittsburgh. I wasn't sure if I wanted to tackle the subject because I didn't know much about the era, but after doing some preliminary research, I was surprised to learn that Prohibition-era Pittsburgh and western Pennsylvania were as violent as other major cities and that here, too, the Noble Experiment led to widespread corruption that lasted long after Prohibition was repealed. Thanks also go to Chad Rhoad and Julia Turner, who saw the work to completion.

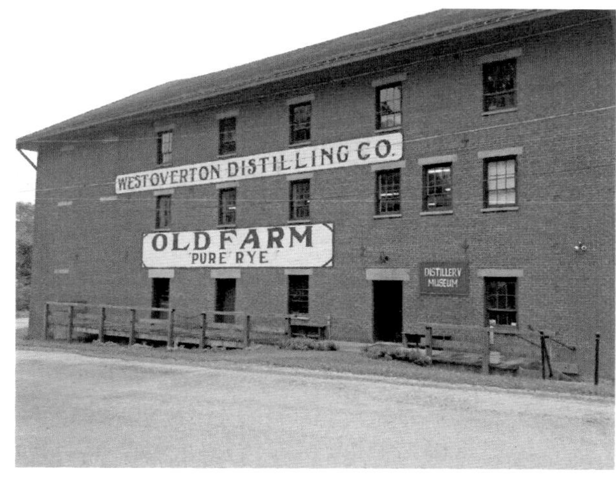

Overton Distilling Co. was once owned by Treasury secretary Andrew Mellon of Pittsburgh, who was charged with enforcing Prohibition laws. *West Overton Museum and Distillery.*

Acknowledgements

Steve Mellon's interactive work on the murders of the Volpe brothers in the *Pittsburgh Post-Gazette* in 2014 served as a roadmap for this book. As with my previous book, my wife, Lucy, was invaluable in making sense out of a manuscript that sometimes meandered far afield.

The records of the Pittsburgh Brewing Co., the Woman's Christian Temperance Union and Henry Clay Frick were useful in providing background, so special thanks also go to the staff at the Archives Service Center at the University of Pittsburgh for their help in retrieving records and photographs. The Pennsylvania Room of the Carnegie Library in Pittsburgh is a good starting place for research, and the staff are always helpful in producing documents and newspaper clippings of the era.

At the West Overton Distillery Museum in Scottdale, Pennsylvania, Stephanie Koller and Logan Holmes were gracious in sharing their information on the history of Old Overholt whiskey and the Overholt family.

Introduction

I was in high school when I came across an old newspaper story about an explosion that ripped apart my grandfather's house in the 1920s. The article attributed the explosion to a faulty coal furnace. I showed the item to my father, who laughed. "The still blew up. Dad was making moonshine in the basement."

Both of my grandfathers liked the taste of moonshine after working long hours hunched over in cold, damp coal mines. I grew up along the Allegheny River in the industrial Allegheny Valley north of Pittsburgh, an area once dotted with coal mines, steel mills, glass factories and foundries. My grandfather Andrew Gazarik emigrated from what is now Slovakia but then was part of the Austro-Hungarian Empire. He came to America and brought his drinking habits with him.

Drinking was part of his life in a grimy, dirt-poor village in Slovakia. He likely drank home-brew called *palenky*, distilled from fruits. He also drank a Slovak gin known as *borovicka* or *hriato*—a beverage made from *palenky*, honey, butter and pork lard—while exchanging toasts of *na zdravie*, "to your health," with his friends.

My maternal grandfather, Zygmunt Maleski, also a coal miner, came from Szylowo, Poland, and probably drank concoctions of Polish moonshine known as *bimber* or *ksiezycowka*. His home was raided during Prohibition by agents who suspected he was operating a still, but the agents had the wrong house. They wanted the home next door.

Whenever my grandfather came home drunk, his three daughters advised my grandmother to "leave *tata* alone. Let him sleep it off." My

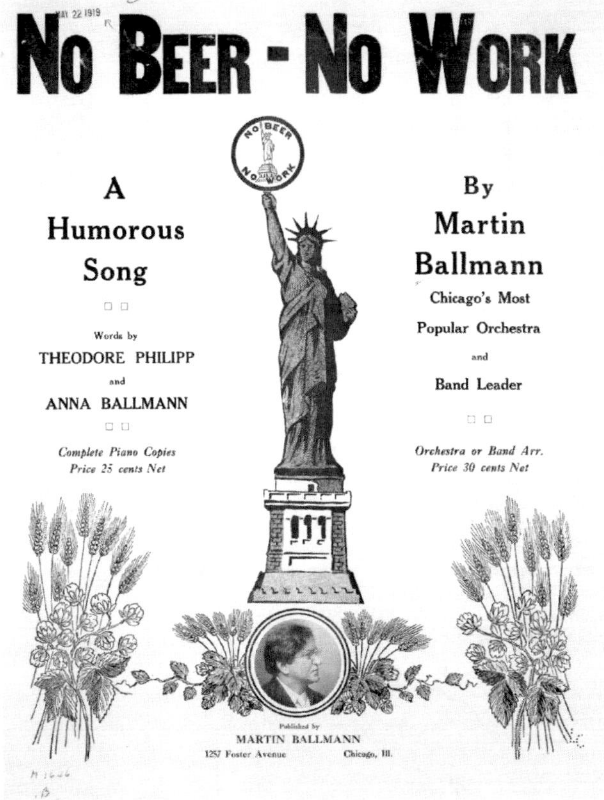

"No Beer— No Work" was a popular Prohibition-era song. *Library of Congress.*

grandmother, a stubborn Pole, disregarded their advice. "She got right up in his face," recalled an uncle. "He liked his booze. He just loved to drink the moonshine." Even though she spent years owning a bar, my grandmother never tasted a drop of liquor in her life.

Pittsburgh saloons were a refuge for immigrant steelworkers and coal miners; there, they could talk to their countrymen in their own tongues and feel at home. Saloons also were a place where workers could escape the drudgery of their jobs. Liquor provided relief from their long days and brutal workweeks.

"The saloon was an oasis and alcohol gave momentary relief from unrelenting toil," wrote S.J. Kleinberg in his study on working-class families.

Congressman Andrew Barchfield of Pittsburgh, who was a physician, said he represented over 100,000 coal miners and steelworkers and resented temperance advocates dictating morals to his constituents.

"These people look upon alcoholic liquor as a right, inborn and God given," said Barchfield in a study commissioned by the Wholesale Liquor

Dealers Association. "What right does a Prohibitionist in Kansas or Alabama or Maine to command a steelworker in my district who faces 2,000-degree Fahrenheit heat at the furnace door that he may not have his beer when his heat is ended?"

During Prohibition, the Protestant-led Anti-Saloon League wanted to transform society by banning saloons and speakeasies and use the law to change social and moral behavior. The mostly Catholic Slavic population believed the law was aimed at Catholicism. One Slovak priest preached that Prohibition was a sin. "I say give the people good food, good fresh air and good wine and beer and whiskey," a priest told the *Pittsburgh Chronicle-Telegram*. "Prohibition is the biggest curse a person can imagine. God will punish this country."

When federal agents in 1930 raided a speakeasy and seized sixty barrels of wine in an immigrant stronghold known as "Skunk Hollow" in the city's Bloomfield neighborhood, they were stoned by a mob before police arrived to rescue them. Agents often faced drunken, hostile patrons when they conducted raids.

Agents had to contend with an irate wife of a saloon owner who accosted them with a chair. At another drinking spot, the patrons formed a human barricade to prevent agents from entering the saloon. After a federal raid on a Strip District speakeasy, angry residents slashed the tires of the agents' cars to show their displeasure.

Protestant ministers protested the Slavs' habit of drinking, dancing and fighting at weddings, christenings and funerals, arguing that ethnic groups held festivities "under the guise of Christianity and the carousing should be abolished if a means can be evolved to carry it out."

Alcohol was as important as food at family gatherings and religious ceremonies. A host was considered inhospitable if he didn't offer his guest a drink on arrival. If a guest rejected a refill, you filled his glass anyway because you knew he was just being polite in rejecting your hospitality.

When someone died, there were toasts to the deceased at the wake. Liquor, said a priest, brought "a little cheer into a dreary house," according to an article in *The Annals of the American Academy of Police and Social Science*. When a relative was married, there was a Slavic tradition in which the men at the reception paid money, knocked back a shot of whiskey and danced briefly with the bride before the next man cut in.

Rural America viewed drinking as a big-city social ill, and temperance advocates viewed saloons as the core of that problem. Money spent on drinking meant less money spent on supporting a family. The saloons, however, were places of refuge for the growing immigrant population,

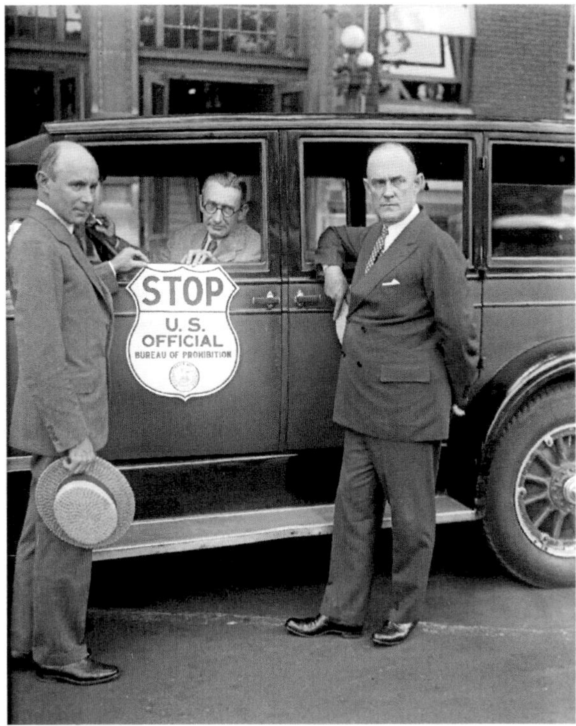

Prohibition Bureau officials pose beside a car used by Prohibition agents. *Library of Congress.*

particularly in western Pennsylvania and Pittsburgh, where the city's population grew from 235,000 in 1880 to more than 670,000 by 1930.

Jews, Italians, Slavs, Russian Orthodox and Roman Catholics arrived here and were looked down on by the wealthy Scotch-Irish Presbyterians who ruled the city financially, economically and culturally. The Scotch-Irish believed poverty was the result of laziness and sin and that drinking was at the root of the problem.

Heavy drinking also occurred in the coal patches that dotted the region surrounding Pittsburgh. There were nearly one hundred killings related to alcohol in these towns during Prohibition, but agents were banned from entering these coal patches by the notorious Coal and Iron Police.

Labor leader Philip Murray, then vice-president of the United Mine Workers Union, blamed the coal companies for allowing "notorious violations" of the Volstead Act in the coal camps.

"Men bootleggers and women bootleggers openly sell liquor in the camps," complained Murray to Pennsylvania lawmakers. "Fights and assaults by drunken men and women no longer attract more than passing attention."

1
The Whiskey Rebellion

Western Pennsylvania sits along the Appalachian Mountain range separating the western part of the state from the east. The mountain's endless ridges, thick forests and rugged landscape, along with its rivers and streams, made it ideal for hiding stills and making moonshine. Even before the Revolutionary War, the region had speakeasies, known as "tippling houses," where thirsty travelers could wet their whistles. Bootleggers were called "tippling house keepers."

Liquor was part of everyday life for the people living along the frontier. Liquor was a symbol of hospitality. Visitors were offered a pull from the jug when they arrived at a neighbor's house. Men drank whiskey at work, before church, at weddings, at baptisms, at funerals, at house-raisings and at harvest time. As part of their daily rations, soldiers were given a gill (a quarter of a pint) of whiskey.

Even clergymen drank. One minister, about to administer confirmation, walked into a Greensburg tavern in Westmoreland County before the ceremony wearing his canonical robes and ordered a tumbler of brandy "without giving offense to the faithful." Clergymen routinely were offered a drink when calling at the homes of their parishioners.

Early nineteenth-century America was a "nation of drunkards," as historian William J. Rorabaugh wrote in *The Alcoholic Republic*. Everybody drank. Doctors, lawyers, laborers, farmhands, the clergy and factory workers all drank regularly during the day. Whiskey was considered medicine. People drank whiskey if they had a fever or were bitten by a snake. Europeans arriving in the United States drank alcohol because water was often dirty or contaminated. If they were thirsty, Americans drank beer to quench their thirst. By 1830, Americans were drinking as much as five gallons of liquor a year.

The Continental Congress was concerned about colonists' excessive drinking and passed a resolution in 1774 encouraging colonial legislatures to enact laws curtailing the distilling of grain. The Methodists and Quakers pushed for curtailment of liquor sales. The Pennsylvania Synod of the Lutheran Church in 1797 ordered ministers to take up the cause of temperance from their pulpits. The Pittsburgh Synod went so far as to decree that alcohol should never be used except for medicinal purposes.

Pittsburgh had two dozen taverns by 1808, with names like the Rising Sun, Semple's Tavern and the Lemon Inn where men drank "slings," "todys" and "bounces" made of whiskey, "cherry" or "jinn." Whiskey was as good as gold in the hardscrabble frontier of western Pennsylvania in the 1790s and was as much a part of the commercial life of the region as it was part of the social. Since hard currency was scarce, farmers used whiskey in place of cash to pay for merchandise or their ministers' salaries.

American whiskey was born in western Pennsylvania, and the region served as the nation's whiskey capital for 150 years, from the 1700s through the 1800s. More than four thousand stills were operating near streams throughout Allegheny, Westmoreland, Fayette and Washington Counties. Colonel Israel Shreve distilled whiskey in Perryopolis. Sam Thompson built a distillery along the Monongahela River in 1844. It closed during Prohibition but emerged after repeal to continue making rye until the middle of the twentieth century.

John Gibson's Son & Company in Belle Vernon started in 1856, but Prohibition forced the company into bankruptcy. Sam Dillinger in Ruffsdale opened his distillery in 1906, producing fifty barrels of rye whiskey a day. Prohibition also put Dillinger out of business, but his company reemerged as Ruffsdale Distilling Company, producing Thos. Moore, Old Possum Hollow, Old Man, Hiram Green, Tom Keene and Old Yock Pure Rye.

The Monongahela River Valley was described in 1811 as a "rich and well-settled country," according to Leland Baldwin's *Whiskey Rebels*. Visitors reported that farmers cultivated wheat, rye, barley, oats, buckwheat, corn and potatoes "in great abundance." It was rye, however, that was used to make whiskey, and Mon Rye was "the best and greatest." Farmers in the fertile valley grew rye that was distilled into whiskey known as Monongahela Rye. "Mon Rye," as it was called, was a sweeter, more robust-tasting whiskey that was allowed to age in barrels rather than swilled as soon as it was made.

Mon Rye was held in such high regard that Herman Melville mentioned the drink in *Moby-Dick*. "'Tis July's immortal fourth; all fountains must run red today! Would now, it revealed New Orleans whiskey or unspeakable old Monongahela!"

Early Pittsburgh was a military outpost filled with rugged frontiersmen, trappers and traders. In 1781, the town was a rural community of four hundred people, but by 1790, Pittsburgh was a bustling city of one thousand. It was slowly transforming itself from a frontier town into a commercial center. Pittsburgh was filled with log homes and muddy streets. It was prospering with ironworks, brickyards, a boatyard, a stone quarry and commercial mills. Flatboats and keelboats plied the Allegheny, Monongahela and Ohio Rivers, which came together at the town.

After the Revolutionary War, a small group of rich men dominated the economy of western Pennsylvania. They bought land and built businesses and industries, creating even more wealth. On the lower end of the economic totem pole were small farmers, who hacked out homesteads in the thick forests of the Appalachian Mountains. Life was hard. For families settling the area, life on the frontier often meant living in poverty. To survive, farmers raised rye or distilled it to make whiskey, which served as currency. A gallon of rye whiskey sold for a quarter, but if a farmer could produce one hundred gallons, he could earn enough money to buy a two-hundred-acre farm near Pittsburgh.

The fledgling United States was a nation struggling to pay its bills. The national debt had reached $830,000 from financing the Revolutionary War. Gold and silver were scarce. The government loaned money to farmers and small business owners but with interest rates that ran as high as 12 percent per month. The cash-strapped farmers were unable to make their payments and often faced foreclosure.

Secretary of the Treasury Alexander Hamilton knew more about finance than anybody in the government or Congress. With the Constitution replacing the Articles of Confederation, Hamilton had the power to levy taxes to finance government operations and to stop states from printing their own paper currencies and issuing bonds. Section 10 of the Constitution also gave the government the authority to call out the militia to enforce federal laws.

Hamilton needed to pay off the national debt and raise revenue to fund the daily expense of running the government. If the government levied a tax on whiskey, it would provide $975,000, which would be more than enough to pay off creditors, but whiskey was currency to the struggling farmers and millers of western Pennsylvania; they believed a whiskey tax was singling them out for punishment. The tax also reeked of the high-handed treatment by the British that led to the Revolution.

Whiskey distillers couldn't ship their product down the Mississippi because the Spanish had closed the river to trade, so that left their only market in the east. Hamilton urged Congress to adopt the tax by using a twofold argument. First, the tax would help the nation survive and pay off its debt. Second, the tax would serve to highlight the public health risk of drinking, hopefully curbing consumption and preventing the country from becoming a nation of sots.

A tax on liquor wasn't something new to the people of western Pennsylvania. In 1684, the colony imposed a tax on whiskey to raise money to fight the French and Indians. Pennsylvania had nineteen laws on the books for taxing liquor, as well as other laws regulating their sale. In 1778, the state passed another law limiting distilling to certain times of the year.

The demand for whiskey was so great that it caused a shortage of grain, which created one of bread. The Pennsylvania legislature in 1756 enacted a whiskey tax, but it wasn't until 1786 that lawmakers implemented a system to collect the money; the measure led to one tax collector, William Graham, being literally run out of the region.

Hamilton wanted farmers to pay $0.09 on each gallon of whiskey they produced. The tax would cost a farmer an average of $1.50 a year at a time when farmers only earned an average of $20.00 annually. Large distillers would pay an annual flat fee based on the capacity of their stills. Before a farmer or distiller could ship the whiskey to market, the stills would have to be registered, and the tax would have to be paid in advance. The tax affected mainly people living in rural areas, where whiskey was used as a medium of exchange because hard currency was scarce.

To distill Monongahela Rye whiskey, a distiller placed corn and rye into a copper kettle and cooked it until it was transformed into mash. A pipe carried the steam from cooking through the lid of the kettle and then into coils known as the worm. A bucket of water was added. The resulting steam became a fluid but was not yet whiskey. As the mash continued to boil, it created an undrinkable liquid. Another boiling process finally created a clear whiskey.

Before the liquor was removed from the still, a government inspector tested each barrel to determine the proof using a hydrometer. Then the name of the distiller, location of the still, the type of liquor, the proof and the number of gallons in each cask would be imprinted on the barrel. Only then would the federal government allow the whiskey to be shipped and sold.

A farmer growing rye could sell his crop for $0.40 a bushel, but if he sold the same crop to a whiskey distiller, he could earn as much as $1.00 on each gallon of whiskey he produced. By 1808, the region was producing a half barrel of whiskey for every person in the nation. Farmers had to register their stills with the government. Failure to do so and pay the tax resulted in exorbitant fines ranging from $150.00 to $200.00, which they were unable to pay.

The tax was collected at stills since they were the point of production, and the payment had to be in coin. If the distillers couldn't pay, the tax collectors seized the whiskey. Each 100 gallons of rye mash made 12 gallons of whiskey. A 100-gallon still produced 1,800 gallons every month for a farmer. If a farmer produced 720 gallons of whiskey over a four-month period, his tax bill would amount to $60.

A farmer could only pack a mule with four bushels of rye grain, but if the rye was distilled into whiskey, a mule could carry the equivalent of twenty-four gallons of liquor to Philadelphia, where it sold for one dollar per gallon.

Two eight-gallon casks could earn a farmer as much as sixteen dollars in the cash-scarce frontier. What the federal government failed to anticipate, however, was the reaction of farmers. There was talk among farmers and distillers of secession and creating a separate state called "Westsylvania" in 1776. In 1784, four counties in North Carolina seceded, creating the Free Republic of Franklin. The unrecognized state survived for four years before rejoining North Carolina after its founder threatened to align Franklin with Spain. Concern grew among farmers that they would be unable to earn enough cash to pay the whiskey tax and would lose their farms to foreclosure.

Imposition of the tax reminded angry farmers of the English tax policies that led to the Revolutionary War. When tax collector Robert Johnson tried to collect the tax, angry farmers shaved his head, poured hot tar over his naked body, rolled him in a pile of goose feathers and left him in the woods. Johnson survived and reported his ordeal to authorities. Angry residents demanded the government repeal the tax and threatened retaliation against anybody who sided with the government.

President Washington grew concerned over the lawlessness in western Pennsylvania and called an emergency cabinet meeting, during which Hamilton urged the president to use force to stem the growing rebellion. General John Neville, a rich distiller, was appointed tax collector for western

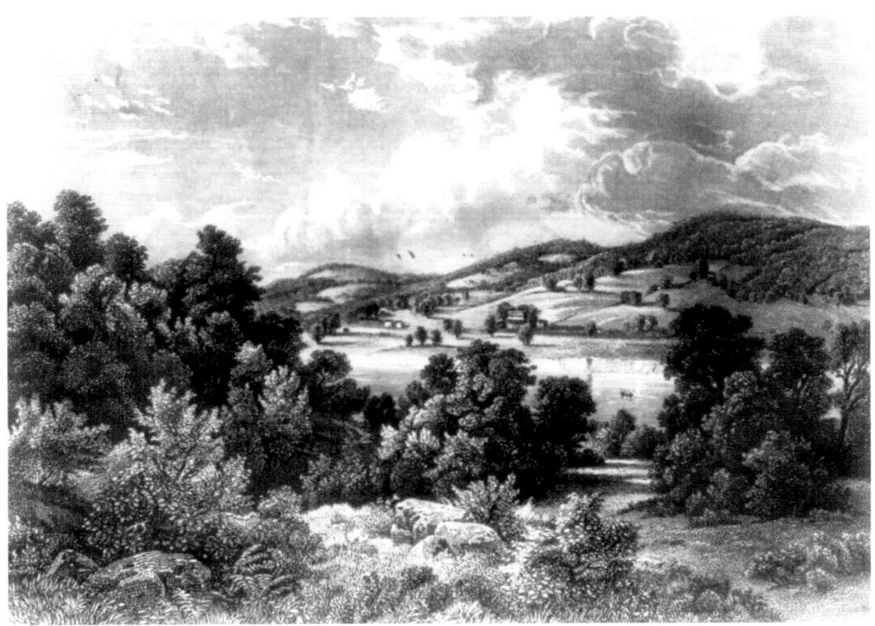

A painting of Braddock's Field along the banks of the Monongahela River, where several thousand whiskey rebels amassed in July 1794, threatening to sack Pittsburgh. *Library of Congress.*

Pennsylvania. He also was the patriarch of a family who had industrial and mercantile interests in the region. When rebels learned of Neville's appointment, they torched his home and began marching on Pittsburgh.

In July 1782, a group of rebellious farmers raised an army of between 5,000 and 6,000 men and massed at Braddock's Field, located nine miles southeast of Pittsburgh. The area was the site of the battle between the French and Indians against British forces led by General Edward Braddock on July 9, 1755. Braddock, accompanied by George Washington, led 1,400 men into the wilderness, where the troops were slaughtered by the French and their native allies. Out of the 1,400 soldiers who marched into battle, 500 were killed, and weapons, artillery, ammunition, food, horses and two hundred gallons of rum were seized as booty.

A group of Pittsburgh militia went out to meet the angry rebels. The two sides stood facing each other, drinking whiskey and firing their muskets into the air. Things were quiet for the night, but the posturing continued the next morning. The rebels were growing impatient; they wanted to march on Pittsburgh and urged their leaders to make a decision. Hugh Henry Brackenridge, a local scholar and lawyer, urged town residents to put out food and whiskey for the rebels and then offered them boats so they could cross the Monongahela River and avoid a confrontation with federal troops.

The rebels marched through Pittsburgh, demanding whiskey at taverns before threatening to burn the city. They held trials for several captured militia leaders and sentenced them to be tarred and feathered before commuting their sentences and forcing them to swear allegiance to the new state of "Westsylvania."

The ragtag army marched on the city but turned back after learning that President Washington was personally leading thirteen thousand soldiers to put down the rebellion, which is considered the nation's first civil war. By the time Washington arrived in Bedford County, the rebellion had petered out in the face of the huge force, and its leaders either fled or were captured. Two were sentenced to hang although they later were pardoned.

Washington was no teetotaler, but he understood the need to suppress the rebellion if the nation was to remain united. He often drank rum punch, porter and whiskey to excess. At his Mount Vernon estate, Washington operated the largest still in the nation at the time. He had five stills encompassing 2,250 square feet when most distilleries were an average of 800 square feet.

After the whiskey rebels retreated to their farms, the stills were registered, but the tax was still difficult to collect. Farmers made moonshine and began smuggling liquor, a practice that would return with Prohibition. Farmers and distillers paid the tax for six years, until Thomas Jefferson became president and repealed it.

2
Temperance Comes to Pittsburgh

Saloons in the late nineteenth and early twentieth centuries were a curse to Pittsburgh clergy and temperance advocates because they were breeding grounds for disease and crime. Men urinated, spit and vomited on floors before passing out and being thrown out onto the street. They were also associated with other forms of vice, such as prostitution.

Carrie A. Nation, the hatchet-swinging grandmother who was the scourge of saloon owners in the early twentieth century, arrived in Pittsburgh in 1904, declaring to the *Pittsburgh Post* that the city was "the worst place I'd ever seen and the saloons are in terrible shape. All the young men in this city are going to hell. The young women, too, are awful, and all this is caused by the saloon."

Nation, whose real name was Carrie Amelia Moore Nation, was arrested shortly after she got off a train in Pittsburgh at the B&O Station. She never got a chance to swing her hatchet. She was arrested for disorderly conduct, for hectoring a man she suspected of being drunk, claiming she smelled alcohol on his breath. "You're mistaken my good woman. I never drank a drop of liquor in my life," said the man.

In the Strip District, there were seventy-eight saloons with names like Hinky Dink, the Stone Jug and the Bucket of Blood. There also were drugstores that sold liquor and private drinking clubs.

As Pittsburgh grew, so did the number of saloons. In 1829, there were 129 saloons in Pittsburgh, plus an additional 162 throughout Allegheny County. The number grew to 289 three years later. Even judges came under scrutiny for their

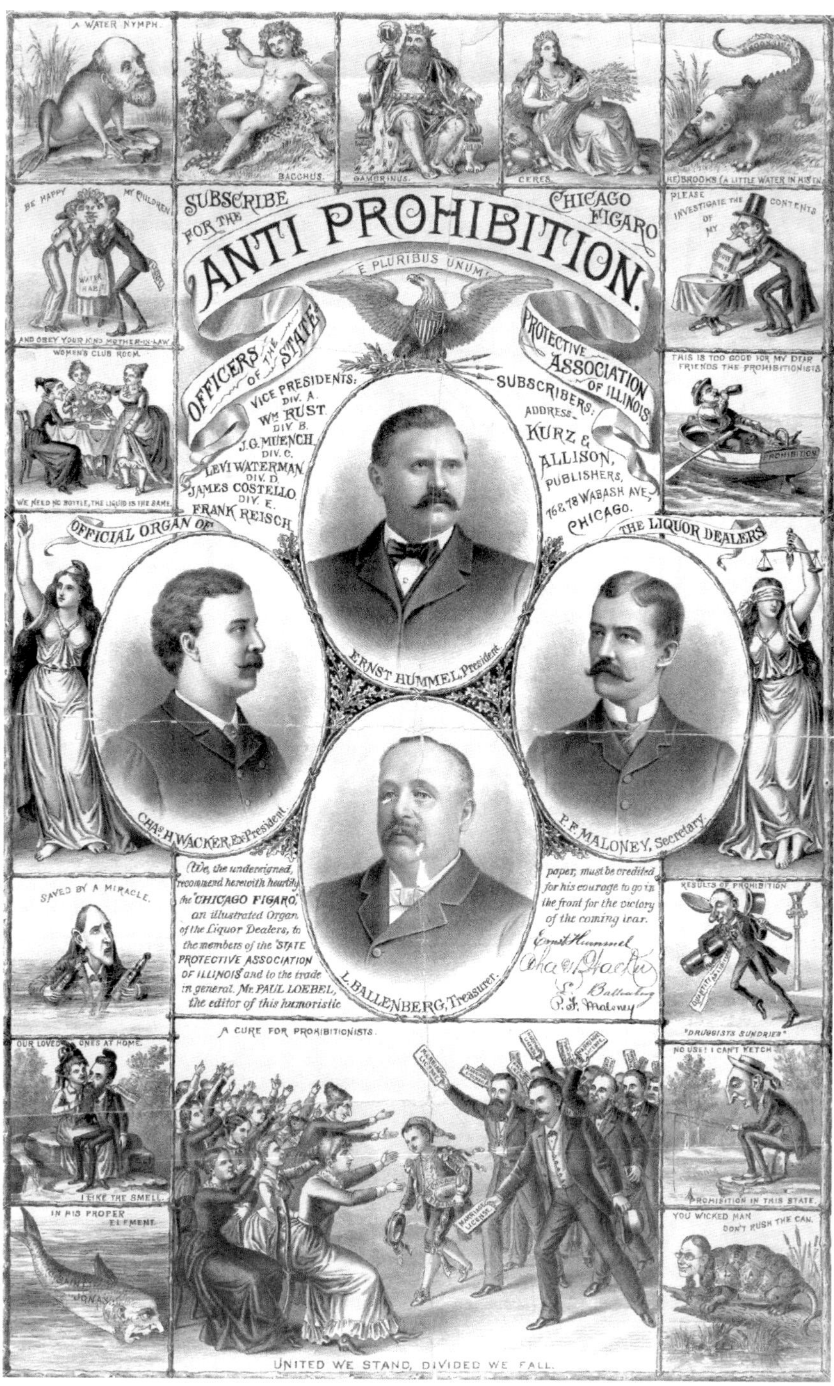

Anti-Prohibition Party poster. *Library of Congress.*

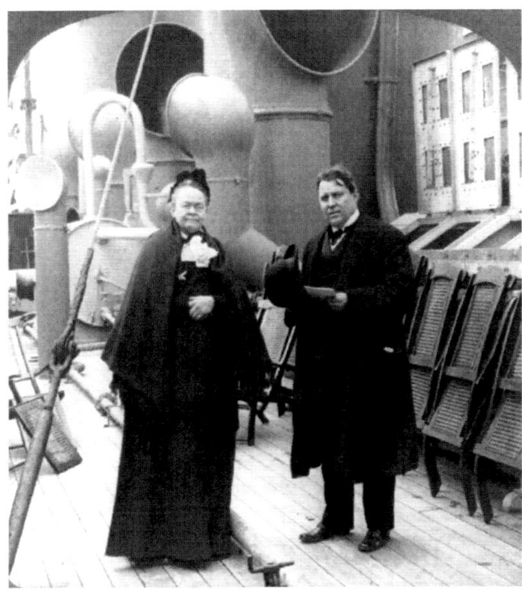

Anti-liquor crusader Carrie A. Nation. *Library of Congress.*

drinking habits. Allegheny County judge Charles Shaler told his fellow jurists that liquor undermines public confidence in the judiciary because "one who belches, rather than utters his judgments, who in losing his sense of shame, loses also his sense of justice," wrote Lloyd L. Sponholtz in *Pittsburgh and Temperance, 1830–1854.*

Efforts to keep Pittsburgh from becoming a city of drunkards began in earnest in 1830 after a proliferation of saloons kept citizens in a constant state of intoxication. Some city blocks had as many as six saloons open. Pittsburghers, like other citizens, were drinking seven gallons of alcohol per capita.

The Pittsburgh Temperance Society was founded on April 26, 1830, and eleven years later, the society was holding marches past saloons with bands, banners and flags. Members lobbied the state legislature to reduce the number of saloon licenses, but the liquor industry responded by threatening to defeat any candidate for political office who sided with the temperance advocates.

By 1836, some hotels in Pittsburgh stopped serving liquor, and a "Temperance Village" was built to house nondrinkers. The Sons of Temperance was created in 1848 and paraded 1,500 members through city streets accompanied by ten bands. The organization had a group for children, the Cadets of Temperance. Once when the cadets were marching, a drunken bystander hanging on a lamppost remarked, "Let's take these little fellows into Weaver's and—*hic*—treat 'em to a drink," according to an account of immigrant drinking habits in *The Annals of the American Academy of Political and Social Science.*

Temperance advocates were thrilled in 1848 when a manufacturing company refused to honor an an order placed by a Pittsburgh distillery needed for making whiskey. "This speaks well for the temperance of those engaged in this branch of the Pittsburgh trade," reported the *Journal of the American Temperance Union*.

Pennsylvania held a statewide temperance referendum in 1854, but Pittsburgh helped defeat the move by a wider vote margin than anywhere else in the state. The legislature made it a crime to provide liquor to anybody who was a known drunkard, a minor or mentally ill. Temperance advocates kept pressure on saloon owners. Lawmakers passed the "jug law" in 1858—banning the sale of liquor in stores and saloons on Sunday—although the law didn't stop them from remaining open.

The Women's Crusade of 1873–74, led by Eliza Daniel Stewart, known as "Mother Stewart," arrived in Pittsburgh from Ohio just as local crusading efforts were foundering. Liquor dealers had spread the word that the crusade was a failure, so Mother Stewart raced to Pittsburgh in time to lead one thousand women on a march to a city park, injecting new vigor into the movement. "Pittsburgh is indeed built on whiskey," Stewart wrote in her autobiography, *Memories of the Crusade: A Thrilling Account of the Great Uprising of the Women of Ohio in 1873 Against the Liquor Crime*.

More than thirty-two thousand women joined the crusade and became a political power even though women could not vote. Before crowds, the crusaders paraded reformed drunks, who regaled listeners with stories of how alcohol had ruined their lives, evoking sympathy from the audience. Women began to employ more radical tactics. Roving bands of women wielding hatchets and axes raided saloons to destroy liquor.

Saloon owners were furious with Mother Stewart, who led prayer meetings outside their establishments in the 1870s, singing and praying and discouraging men from entering. Men at the saloons jeered and heckled the women, who asked the beer-guzzling customers to sign the abstinence pledge.

Liquor dealers persuaded the mayor to remove the women, and he ordered two police officers to arrest Stewart and her followers. A mob surrounded the policemen to prevent the arrests, but Mother Stewart mounted a whiskey barrel, appealing for calm. Then she led thirty-two temperance crusaders, marching two abreast behind the police officers, off to the city jail, which could not hold all the women. A judge ordered the women released, saying they had committed no crime. They were arrested two more times, but on the third time, several of the group were placed in the police lockup, where they marched up and down the corridor singing and praying until the police couldn't stand the noise any longer and released them.

The *Gazette Times* in Pittsburgh reported the Woman's Christian Temperance Union complained about the use of liquor in candy. "Pittsburgh is behind New

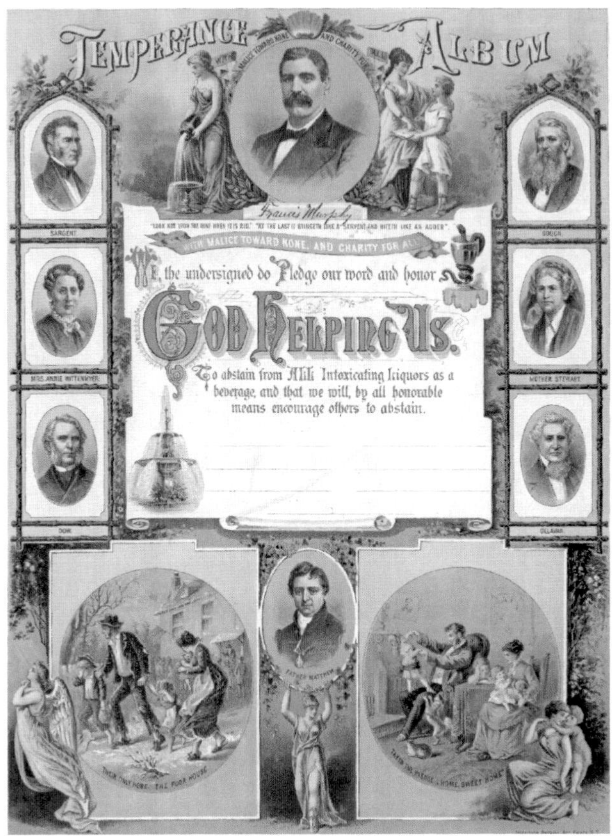

A poster with the oath of abstinence promoted by the Woman's Christian Temperance Union. *Library of Congress.*

York in taking care of this phase of the liquor question and I think it's time we began to look into it."

In 1887, the Pennsylvania General Assembly passed the Brooks Law, which increased the price of a liquor license by an average of $100 a year. To obtain a state license, an applicant had to prove there was a demand for another saloon in the neighborhood and that the owner could generate enough business to warrant a license. In the late nineteenth century, there were over 1,300 saloons in Pittsburgh. The fee for a license within the city was $1,000 and outside the city, $500. By 1892, there were more than 50 saloons in Homestead, which is located across the Monongahela River from Pittsburgh. Homestead, the site of the famous streel strike, had a population of twenty-five thousand and had as many as 8 saloons to a block.

Despite the high fees, Pittsburgh clergy charged it was still too easy to obtain a saloon license because, they claimed, the judiciary was in bed with the saloon owners and the liquor industry. Ministers said judges were all too eager to grant licenses and claimed the licensing hearings were a fraud because critics were kept out of the courtroom. The Brooks Law, argued the clergymen, allowed more women to drink in saloons by giving them a separate entrance through a back door. They said women were becoming more brazen in their drinking habits.

"They take beer, wine and mixed drinks with their lunches and dinners at restaurants and cafés and stop for a glass of wine or anything else they want on the way to the theater," said a minister. "From early morning until midnight you will find women and girls sitting around in the places, drinking beer and gossiping to others," complained the WCTU.

Pittsburgh's problems with speakeasies existed long before Prohibition. In the 1890s, police, reacting to complaints from clergy, raided speakeasies on Sundays, when business was the busiest. The joints sold warm beer "while the whiskey is relentless as death."

Professor Alexander Schoeb, a music teacher, operated a speakeasy that served wine and champagne, according to an 1891 article in the *New York Times*. Drugstores sold whiskey "strong enough to take the hair off a dog" from midnight to 3:00 a.m. at a dime a shot, according to the *Times*. Bootleggers sold liquor at carnivals, fairs and auctions. These dealers were known as "walking

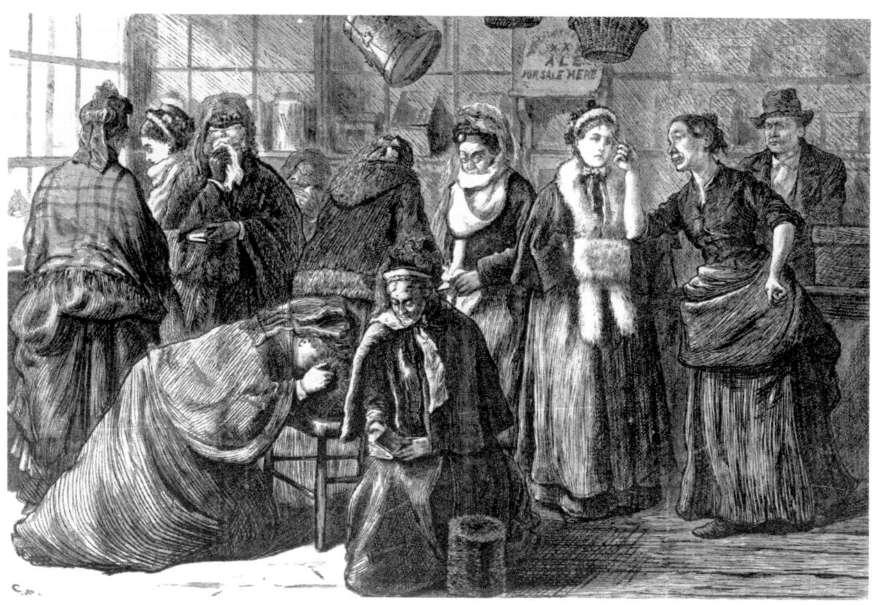

Temperance crusaders went into a Pittsburgh saloon, fell to the floor and prayed while drunken customers ridiculed them. *Library of Congress.*

speakeasies" because they strolled through the crowd, attracting customers.

One of the wettest neighbors of the city was the Strip District, which was known as the "hog trough" of the city. By 1915, there were ninety-six saloons and speakeasies in the neighborhood, which was only three-fifths of a square mile wide. "No one need go alcoholistically thirsty in the Strip," reported the Christian Social Service Union. "Drunkeness is rampant and the district is polluted. Husbands and fathers drinking, carouse while their wives labor to support needy children." The growth of these neighborhood watering holes was aided by liquor interests that underwrote mortgages for saloon owners.

Many of the establishments were owned by city politicians, who employed the police to keep order in their bars. Men literally drank themselves to death in these dives. Men often were found suffering from delirium tremens or alcohol poisoning and died on the spot.

Historical Temperance Songs

ARRANGED FOR INSTITUTES

East End W. C. T. U.
Allegheny County, Pa.

Psalm 146, The Crusade Psalm.
Give to the Winds Thy Fears.
Crusade Hymn.
Saloons Must Go.
A Saloonless Nation in 1920.
Some Glad Day.
Ratified.
Obey the Law.
Work for Enforcement Where You Are
Hold Fast and Go Forward.
The More We Get Together.
Carry On.
That New Member.
Eternal Vigilance Is the Price.
Look Ahead.
It Is There to Stay.
The World Is Going Dry.
Beautiful Hour of Noontide.
Temperance Doxology.

This page and opposite: Songs of the Woman's Christian Temperance Union. *Archives Service Center, University of Pittsburgh.*

Temperance evangelist Francis Murphy was persuaded to come to Pittsburgh in 1876 to aid the local movement. Murphy claimed more than eighty thousand signed the pledge before he left after a year of preaching. Frances Willard came to Pittsburgh, where she launched the Woman's Christian Temperance Union. One day in 1874, she walked into Sheffner's saloon reading from Psalms and then dropped to her knees on the sawdust-covered floor and began singing

TEMPERANCE SONGS

For God and Home and Every Land

Time of Prayer—Noontide

"It is always noontide somewhere,
And across the awakening continents
From shore to shore, somewhere,
Our prayers are rising evermore."

That New Member

Mrs. Howard Teasdale

Tune, "Coming Through the Rye"

Have you got her, that new member
For our temperance band?
Have you got her, that new member
To help free our land?
Have you got her, that new member
To protect our youth?
Have you got her, that new member
To help spread the truth?

Temperance Doxology

Tune—Old Hundred

Praise God, from whom all blessings flow;
Praise Him, who saves from deepest woe;
Praise Him who leads the temperance host
Praise Father, Son and Holy Ghost.

Eternal Vigilance is the Price

(Tune: "Yankee Doodle")

Eternal Vigilance is the price,
The price of prohibition
You dare not weaken nor give up,
'Till victory's completion.

CHORUS:

Get the Slogan on your heart
Give it contemplation;
Eternal Vigilance is the price,
The price of Prohibition.

Wake up, get up, stay up and work
For greater prohibition.
We'll win the day, yes, come what may,
Because of your devotion.

H. L. B.

Obey the Law!

Tune—Maryland, My Maryland

The call is ringing, far and wide,
"Obey the law!" "Obey the law!"
From city, town and countryside,
"Obey the law!" "Obey the law!"

And loyal patriots, one and all
Lest ill our country should befall,
Will promptly answer to the call,
"Obey the law!" "Obey the law!"

Our Constitution now maintain,
"Obey the law!" "Obey the law!"
Till justice everywhere shall reign,
In public life and private, too,
We call for men with vision true,
Who'll dare this vital thing to do,
"Obey the law!" "Obey the law!"

Rev. C. E. Nichols.

The More We Get Together

(Tune: "Augustine")

The more we work together, together, together,
The more we work together, the better 'twill be.
For your work helps my work, and my work helps your work,
The more we work together, the better 'twill be.

The more we pray together, together, together,
The more we pray together, the stronger we'll be.
For your faith helps my faith, and my faith helps your faith,
The more we pray together, the stronger we'll be.

The more we vote together, together, together,
The more we vote together, the drier we'll be.
For my votes are dry votes, and your votes are dry votes,
The more we vote together, the drier we'll be.

MRS. S. R. B. STEWART, 613 Hampton Avenue, Wilkinsburg, Pa.

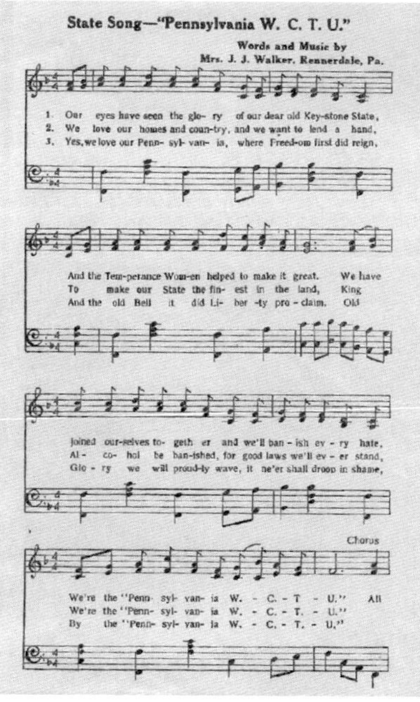

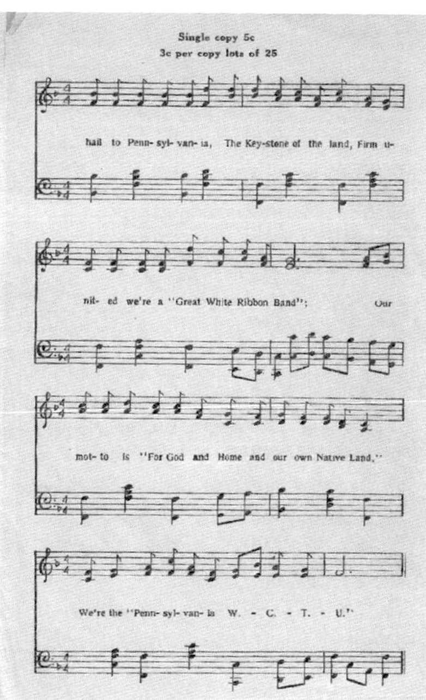

"Rock of Ages." The bar was filled with dirty, rough-looking men who jeered and heckled her and the women with her.

Saloons weren't the only place Willard had a hard time reaching. Some churches refused to let her preach. "Frances Willard, noble soul, was refused permission to speak from the pulpit of a Methodist Protestant Church because the pastor felt she might desecrate the sacred desk," according to a history of the movement in Pittsburgh.

Billy Sunday, a former baseball player with the Pittsburgh Alleghenys, returned to the city and established a Glory Barn in the Oakland section proclaiming Satan's greatest evil was alcohol. He spent fifty-six days preaching to large crowds that alcohol was a tool used by Satan to force people to commit sin and wanted saloons closed. Sunday joined with the Anti-Saloon League in 1908 and officiated at the funeral of John Barleycorn in Norfolk, Virginia.

"Goodbye John Barleycorn," Sunday proclaimed. "You were God's worst enemy," he said. "You were hell's best friend. I hate you with perfect hatred," reported the *New York Times* in 1920.

Liquor dealers in Allegheny County protested Sunday's appearance, accusing the evangelist of "poisoning the minds of the people against our business and all engaged in it by his clownish antics and lying tirade of abuse and vituperation delivered during these revival meeting," reported the *Gazette Times*.

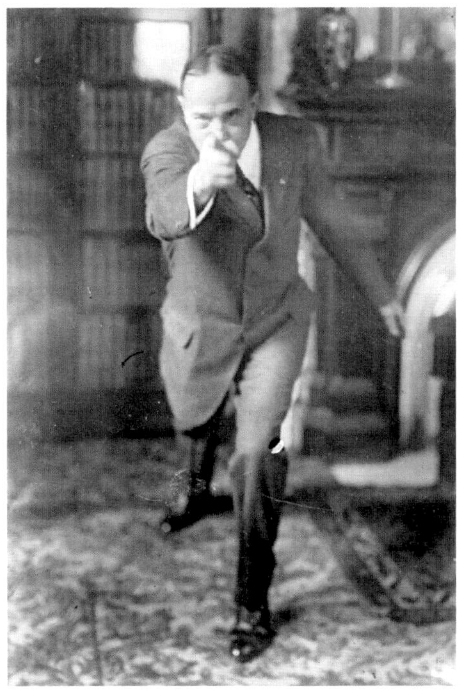

Billy Sunday preached about the evils of alcohol in Pittsburgh, where he once played professional baseball. *Library of Congress.*

The owners of Sunday's former team, now called the Pittsburgh Pirates, included clauses in players' contracts requiring them to abstain from alcohol during the season. Their contracts prohibited them from drinking anything stronger than egg sherry or ice cream sundaes. Pirates president Barney Dreyfuss believed "sobriety and total abstinence is the best course for athletes to pursue,"

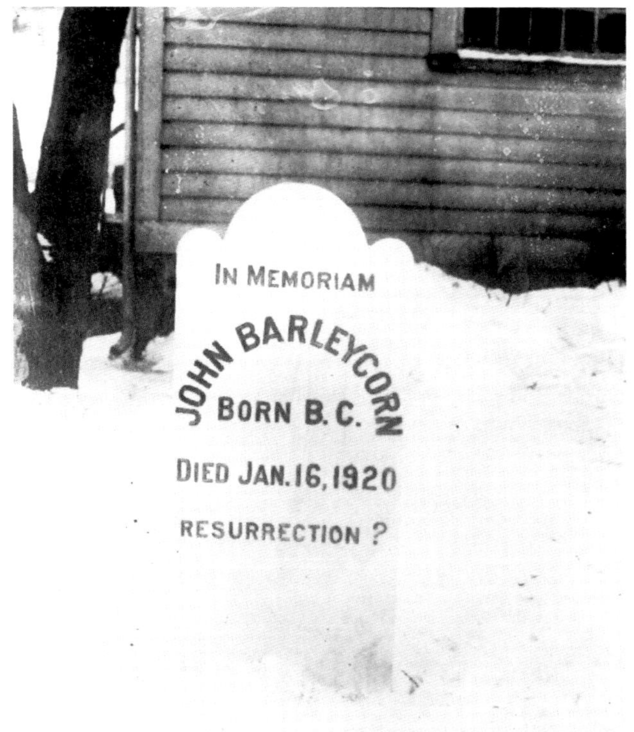

The epitaph for John Barleycorn. *Library of Congress.*

according to an article in the University of Pennsylvania *Journal of Labor Law and Employment.*

The powerful Anti-Saloon League was formed in 1893, a time when there was one saloon for every two hundred Pittsburgh residents. The league grew into a powerful lobbying organization by aligning itself with the clergy, church officials and Sunday school teachers to push for Prohibition. The league made outlandish claims to support its arguments, including that there were fifteen thousand people in Pennsylvania mental hospitals suffering from mental illness caused by alcohol.

The Reverend Dr. George Hodges, rector of the Calvary Episcopal Church in Pittsburgh in 1889, began to preach a social gospel aimed at reforming corrupt government and care of the underprivileged. Since saloons were the base of political bosses' support in machine politics, Hodges targeted saloons in need of reform. The Anti-Saloon League, led by the powerful Wayne Wheeler, became a quasi-police force. It hired private detectives to gather evidence against saloon owners to use in court.

"Saloons are built and stocked and managed and multiplied not to minister to the normal thirst of the community but to increase it for the purpose of making money," said Hodges, according to Keith A. Zahniser in *Steel City Gospel.*

Not all Protestant churches were advocates of Prohibition. The Episcopal Church released a study in 1928 arguing morality could not be legislated. "Prohibition, in itself, is morally wrong and violates fundamental moral principles," said the Reverend W. Fred Allen of Philadelphia in "Preachers on Prohibition as We See It." Allen said churches didn't have any right to force Prohibition on anybody, arguing it was "the most complete and humiliating confession of failure which the church has ever made," he added.

William L. King was an attorney for the Anti-Saloon League when the Citizens League of Pittsburgh and Allegheny County hired him in 1926 to run the organization. King turned out to be a scoundrel. A year later, King fled the city after taking more than $30,000 in bribes from bootleggers and the liquor interests. The league eventually forgave King, and he returned to Pittsburgh and his job as the league's director to begin concocting evidence in liquor prosecutions.

He was indicted by a grand jury for conspiring to obtain false indictments against bootleggers and saloon operators after he filed charges in thirty-four cases based on false evidence. He doctored sales receipts to make it appear that defendants charged with liquor law violations had purchased liquor illegally when they hadn't. King vanished along with the evidence investigators had gathered against bootleggers.

"He sold us out," a committee member told the *Pittsburgh Post-Gazette.*

3

Prohibition

Prohibition is an awful flop.
We like it.
It can't stop what it's meant to stop.
We like it.
It's left a trail of graft and slime,
It's filled our land with vice and crime,
It don't prohibit worth a dime,
Nevertheless, we're for it.
—*Franklin P. Adams,* New York World

The Lever Food Control Act gave the federal government the power to shut off the taps during World War I to conserve grains for troops fighting in Europe by banning the production of alcohol from wheat, corn, rye, yeast and sugar to aid the war effort. Giving up beer and whiskey seemed like a patriotic thing to do since hysteria had made Americans view German American brewers as enemies of the state.

The government also limited the amount of alcohol that could be added to beer by reducing its content to 2.75 percent during the war. After the war's end, the alcohol content of this "near bear" was further reduced to 0.5 percent. Breweries tried to remain in business by producing other products, such as ice cream. One cereal-based liquid was known as "Bevo," which tasted like beer but contained no alcohol. Bootleggers purchased Bevo and then "juiced" it by adding alcohol.

Pennsylvania's rotund Senator Boise Penrose predicted wartime prohibition would be lifted by the end of 1919 if not sooner when the armistice ending World War I was ratified, and ratification, Penrose boasted, would come "sooner than anybody now anticipated," reported the *Pittsburgh Press*. Penrose was off by thirteen years. No American would be able to legally drink a sip of whiskey or beer until 1933.

The Eighteenth Amendment was ratified on December 18, 1917, and became effective on January 17, 1920. The National Prohibition Act of 1919 was enacted, giving the federal and state governments parallel enforcement powers, although the states hoped the federal government would take the lead in enforcing the measure.

Pittsburgh officially went on the wagon at 11:45 p.m. on June 30, 1919, when President Woodrow Wilson refused to lift the wartime ban on booze, arguing that only Congress had the authority. Even weak beer with 2.75 percent alcohol was prohibited. By then, temperance forces had gained political control of Congress to push for the Eighteenth Amendment.

In 1914, the Anti-Saloon League had tried to push the Eighteenth Amendment through Congress, but the attempt failed because of lack of public support. By January 1920, with the war ended, the drys had grown into a powerful political force by helping elect like-minded candidates to Congress. The league controlled two-thirds of the votes in the House and Senate and had the influence to persuade lawmakers to adopt the amendment, which was then sent to the states for ratification.

The Eighteenth Amendment spawned the National Prohibition Act, commonly known as the Volstead Act. The law allowed the government to seize sixty-nine million gallons of liquor stored in bonded warehouses across the United States. More than $1 billion worth of liquor was kept in western Pennsylvania, out of reach of consumers, along with lost tax revenue. Liquor dealers and saloonkeepers had to dispose of their stocks or face confiscation by the government. As soon as the law went into effect, revenue agents began rounding up violators. More than thirty thousand agents fanned out across the nation, making five hundred arrests.

The Volstead Act, named after an obscure Minnesota congressman, Andrew Volstead, was ratified on January 29, 1919. The real power behind the legislation, however, was Morris Sheppard, a congressman and later senator from Texas, who became known as the "father of national Prohibition." In her book *Bootleg: Murder, Moonshine, and the Lawless Years of Prohibition*, Karen Blumenthal wrote that Sheppard believed "the liquor traffic is a peril to society. I shall oppose this scourge from hell until my arm can strike no longer and my tongue can speak no more."

President Wilson vetoed the Volstead Act, but the House and Senate overrode his veto and the act became the law of the land. A proposal to amend the U.S. Constitution to ban alcohol had been discussed as early as

1913. Prohibition advocates knew they were confronting a powerful lobby in the brewing and distilling industries. In 1916, a federal grand jury in Pittsburgh indicted 110 brewers under the United States and Pennsylvania Brewing Associations for financing the campaigns of politicians by amassing a $2 million slush fund.

The indictments included seventy-three Pennsylvania breweries, including three in Pittsburgh. The Fort Pitt Brewing Co., the Duquesne Brewing Co. and the Independent Brewing Co. were accused of financing the campaigns of one U.S. senator and thirty-six congressmen in the 1914 elections. The power of the associations was such that it sidetracked two hundred bills the groups believed were harmful to the beer industry.

Though shunted aside during Prohibition, the brewers continued to be a political force, financing campaigns of lawmakers who favored repeal. With the sale of liquor banned, bootleggers filled the vacuum left by the liquor industry. Their influence began at the top of the political food chain with the mayor and worked its way down to ward bosses, precinct captains and police, who all were part of the corruption that prevailed in Pittsburgh for more than a decade. In 1928, a Pittsburgh congressman was reelected despite being convicted of using his political connections to secure the release from the government of four thousand cases of whiskey.

In the early days of Prohibition, Pittsburgh was "wringing wet," and "Pennsylvania is very wet and only the price is needed by those who want whiskey and plenty of it," said a government report. Prohibition agents scoured western Pennsylvania after the law went into effect, hunting for contraband liquor. U.S. attorney John D. Meyer of Pittsburgh tried to recruit an army of informers to gather intelligence on bootleggers.

"If necessary, I will put a spy on every door step in Pittsburgh," he told the *Pittsburgh Press*.

Most hotels in Pittsburgh sold off their liquor stocks as Prohibition neared, but a few, like the upscale William Penn Hotel, continued to cater to thirsty guests. The hotel's managers opened a bar beneath the lobby that had a secret escape route into downtown in the event of a federal raid. Ironically, the hotel was the meeting place for Prohibition advocates such as the Dry Federation of Pennsylvania. It also was the place where Pittsburgh's Prohibition administrator John Pennington delivered a farewell address before his transfer to Philadelphia.

The hotel is now known as the Omni William Penn, and management has reopened the speakeasy into a plush nightspot with a 1920s atmosphere. The former Nixon Theater in downtown also had a speakeasy in the back of the theater known as the "Flying Squadron," where jazz singer Helen Morgan sat atop a piano entertaining customers.

Twenty-four hours after Prohibition became law, agents raided a speakeasy near Pittsburgh in Homestead, seizing eight hundred gallons of alcohol. Agents went from saloon to saloon armed with search warrants. They seized a four-truck convoy containing $70,000 worth of whiskey headed from Indiana, Pennsylvania, to Pittsburgh. Agents seized one hundred barrels of beer in Westmoreland County destined for Pittsburgh. Agents discovered two thousand barrels of beer in rural Somerset County and dumped poison into the vats to discourage anyone from drinking it.

Frustrated bootleggers created their own detective bureau shadowing and trailing Prohibition agents as they left their Pittsburgh office on raids. They also tried to infiltrate the Prohibition Bureau by having their cronies apply for jobs as Prohibition agents so the bootleggers would know in advance about raids and who was being targeted.

Near Erie, residents of Corry applauded fifty federal agents as they raided twenty speakeasies, making the town "as dry as a cocktail shaker on the morning after." They seized hundreds of gallons of liquor and arrested fourteen men and women. To show their appreciation, Corry residents held a picnic for the agents.

Bootleggers were desperate to get their hands on pre-Prohibition liquor any way they could. In early 1920, police arrested fifteen men in the process of stealing $200,000 worth of liquor from train cars that had stopped in Pittsburgh en route from Kentucky to New York City. Thieves had cut holes in the roof of the cars and were hauling away 849 cases of liquor when they were nabbed.

Warehouses became a prime target of bootleggers. In 1920, more than twelve million gallons of liquor disappeared from warehouses across the country. There were sixty-two bonded warehouses in Pennsylvania holding fifty million gallons of liquor. Whiskey began disappearing from bonded warehouses in western Pennsylvania as soon as Prohibition went into effect. Thieves used counterfeit government permits to steal liquor or broke into warehouses and hauled the booze away on trucks. They created fictitious companies and made bogus rubber stamps and stationery to trick guards.

In a five-month period in 1920, thirteen warehouses in western Pennsylvania were robbed of more than $1 million worth of liquor by organized rings operating in Pittsburgh. When thieves couldn't use deception to remove the liquor, they broke into the warehouses. In Fayette County, south of Pittsburgh, bootleggers tore off the steel doors of one warehouse and made off with $125,000 worth of whiskey. Even though the liquor's owners no longer had possession of their stock, they still were liable to the government for the tax on every stolen gallon.

During a raid by federal agents in Fayette County, agents got into a gun battle with thieves when they interrupted a warehouse robbery in progress. In January 1921, agents got into another shootout with hijackers attempting to steal $100,000 in liquor from a railroad car in Uniontown.

A Pittsburgh businessman told police he was offered a bounty of two dollars per case if he could obtain a government permit for twenty thousand cases. Bootleggers also purchased government letterhead and rubber stamps to deceive guards at warehouses. The U.S. Secret Service arrested a group of men in Pittsburgh who owned a printing shop that made counterfeit government liquor tax stamps. During a search of their shop, agents found more than twenty-five thousand stamps. Herman Lehman, a Northside saloon owner, was caught during a raid with thirty-one cases of bonded whiskey that had been removed from a government warehouse but claimed he was unable to explain how he obtained the liquor.

Sometimes the liquor stored in warehouses didn't have to be stolen. It just mysteriously vanished. In 1923, a Pittsburgh distillery discovered fifty thousand gallons of whiskey had disappeared without the required government permits. Agents suspected it ended up in the hands of bootleggers, who could charge top prices for the good-quality liquor.

Some bootleggers even opened drugstores so they could obtain medicinal whiskey. They would rent storefronts, put up a sign, stock the shelves and then apply for a government permit. In Pittsburgh, there were nearly three hundred physicians granted special prescription pads to prescribe liquor to patients. More than eleven thousand gallons were prescribed in the Pittsburgh region in 1930.

Medicine in the eighteenth century classified liquor as a medicine, claiming it had nutritional value because it contained vitamins. An exception to the Volstead Act allowed physicians to prescribe whiskey, brandy and beer for a variety of ailments, including tuberculosis, pneumonia and high blood pressure. The American Medical Association sided with temperance advocates, adopting a resolution that alcohol has no scientific value as medicine "and should be further discouraged."

Another technique used by smugglers was to forge the names of druggists who were allowed to dispense prescribed whiskey for illness. After one raid, agents found thirty cases of whiskey with numbers that matched a shipment taken from a government warehouse.

In 1922, agents in Pittsburgh arrested two druggists and a man named Jack Branch who were behind a nationwide whiskey smuggling network that stole liquor from warehouses. Pittsburgh Prohibition director John Enciosis called Branch "the biggest bootlegger in the United States" at the time. He used forged permits to remove the liquor from facilities in Pennsylvania, New York, New Jersey and Delaware. The permits always limited the shipments to fourteen cases because any amount over fifteen

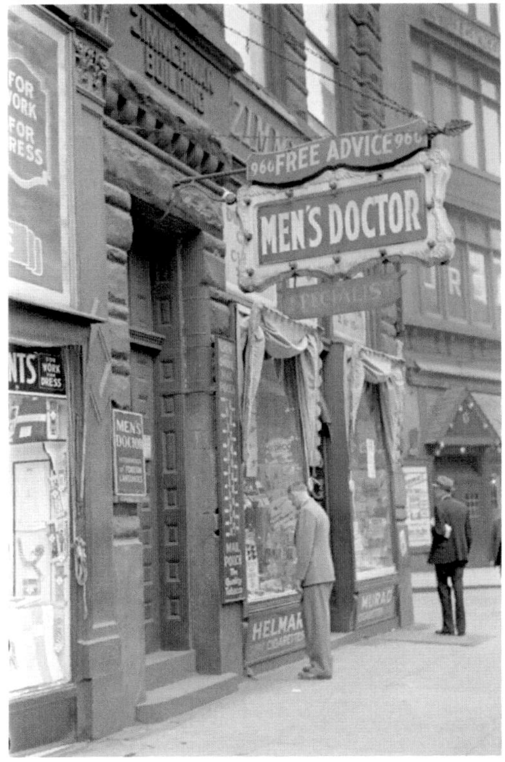

A phony doctor's office where "patients" could get prescriptions for medicinal alcohol. *Library of Congress.*

cases required government confirmation.

Speakeasy owners tried everything to get their hands on liquor shipments. In 1927, agents intercepted a shipment of rags containing 1,200 bottles of French cognac that had been shipped from France to Pittsburgh.

Most of the liquor confiscated by federal agents was made within twenty miles of Pittsburgh. Bootleggers could make several different types from one batch of alcohol just by adding some flavoring and bottling it with different labels.

Frederick Baird, Prohibition administrator for Pennsylvania, explained to a Senate subcommittee in 1926 how Pittsburgh bootleggers were able to convert a pint of rye whiskey into five pints. By adding water and caramel coloring to alcohol, they could bottle the "rye" and sell five pints instead of one.

Bootleg chemists were able to reduce poisonous wood alcohol from 5.00 percent to a safe 1.00 percent and by adding water further reduce the toxicity level to 0.05 percent. Then they would take the denatured wood alcohol; add water, flavoring and a color additive; and produce gin. A drink known as "Pittsburgh Scotch" was made from denatured wood alcohol, creosote and caramel coloring.

Some speakeasies sold low-potency beer that was "juiced" with alcohol to give it a kick. Others sold potent forms of moonshine branded as "white mule" or "third rail liquor." Each week, thirty railroad cars, secretly carrying shipments of beer among their cargo, arrived in Pittsburgh. Bootleggers paid twenty dollars a barrel and then sold the beer for fifty dollars a barrel to speakeasy operators.

4

Gangsters, Guns and Corruption

As passage of the Volstead Act neared, liquor dealers and saloon owners sold off their stocks before they would allow Prohibition agents to confiscate them. Prices soared. A case of whiskey sold for thirty-six dollars. One dealer stacked cases of booze twelve feet high on the sidewalk in front of his establishment, selling twelve thousand quarts of whiskey in one day.

With Prohibition came violence, and with violence came corruption. In the Hazelwood neighborhood of Pittsburgh, federal agents seized $300,000 worth of liquor after private detectives hired by the Anti-Saloon League gathered evidence of bootlegging. Members of the Hazelwood Enforcement League complained that police refused to crack down on speakeasies operating openly in the neighborhood. The *Pittsburgh Post-Gazette* reported that Pittsburgh ministers complained that the police were not enforcing the law. "Pittsburgh ranks very low in the enforcement of the Prohibition amendment," said the Reverend Dr. C.R. Zahniser. "Matters are bad here."

There were 900 police officers on the force in Pittsburgh in 1928. There were another 2,700 in communities surrounding the city, yet the combined forces only made 43 arrests in a four-month period compared to 362 by federal agents during the same period.

The end of the war and the demobilization of thousands of jobless soldiers, sailors and marines triggered a crime wave that police seemed powerless to stop. Murders went unsolved. Highway robberies were frequent. A Pittsburgh beat cop was beaten unconscious. There was a rash of car thefts. Criminals operated with impunity.

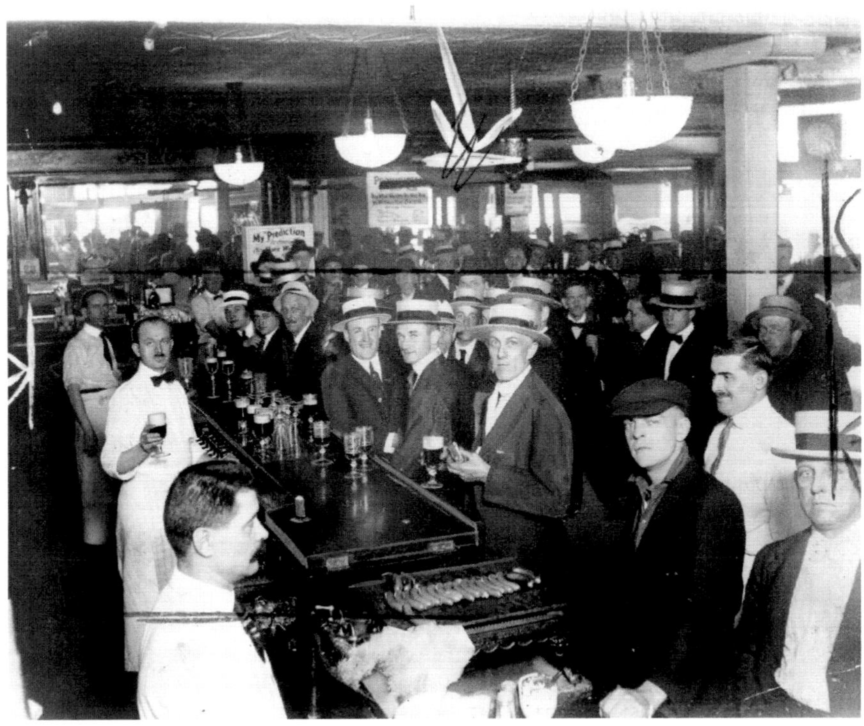

Glum saloon patrons wait for last call before the start of Prohibition. *Library of Congress.*

Corruption seeped into government. South of Pittsburgh in rural Fayette County, Constable John Donohoe of Uniontown, who was a bootlegger and former state trooper, was shot twelve times on July 31, 1929. Donohoe had made a number of enemies, including two county judges, several attorneys and a state trooper. He told acquaintances that he planned vengeance against his enemies who were trying to remove him as constable.

Donohoe accused police of protecting liquor shipments being trucked from Connellsville to nearby Uniontown. Liquor proved a financial boon to Donohoe, who was known for hosting lavish dinner parties. Detectives initially suspected Ed "Big Ed" Wonsetler of killing Donohoe after Wonsetler admitted paying $700 in protection to local officials. State police arrested a number of suspects, which resulted in their subsequent release.

Tony Bell, a former county detective, was charged with the murder but was acquitted by a jury in 1930. Two years later, Bell was arrested for extortion and confessed to investigators he was one of four men who killed Donohoe because the constable kept payoff money from racketeers destined

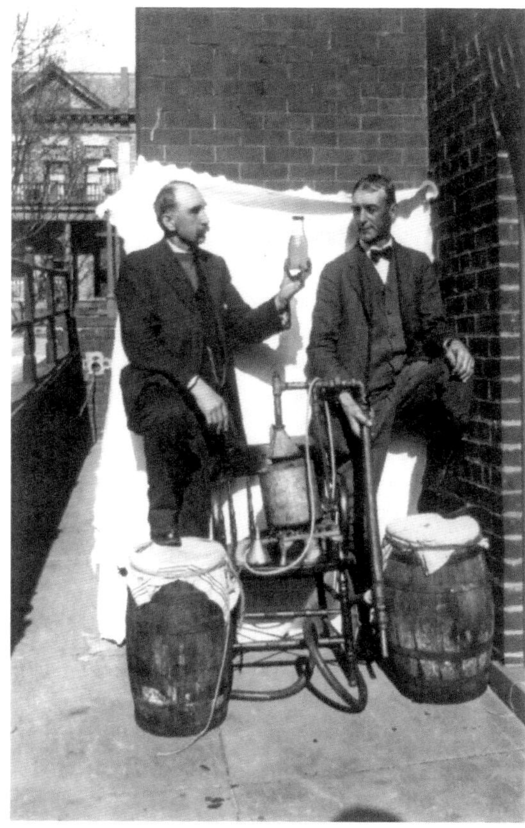

Small home stills allowed residents to distill their own moonshine. *Library of Congress.*

for county politicians. Bell could not be charged since he was protected by double jeopardy, but he implicated three other men in the slaying.

Federal agents, who only were allowed to use their weapons to protect themselves, engaged in a fifteen-mile running gun battle with bootleggers in Fayette County. The two sides exchanged fifty shots before the suspects abandoned their vehicle and fled into the woods.

Speakeasy operators and federal agents waged guerrilla war. After the supply of pre-Prohibition liquor was exhausted and bootleggers started making their own whiskey, the air in Pittsburgh was filled with the odor of mash. Agents were able to obtain "smell warrants" to trace the source of the aroma. Pittsburgh's first Prohibition administrator, Frederick C. Baird, said there were ten thousand stills operating in the city and in Allegheny County by 1926.

Every drop was precious. Bootleggers steamed the last drops of moonshine out of the wood of barrels, creating an aroma that wafted into the air. Agents

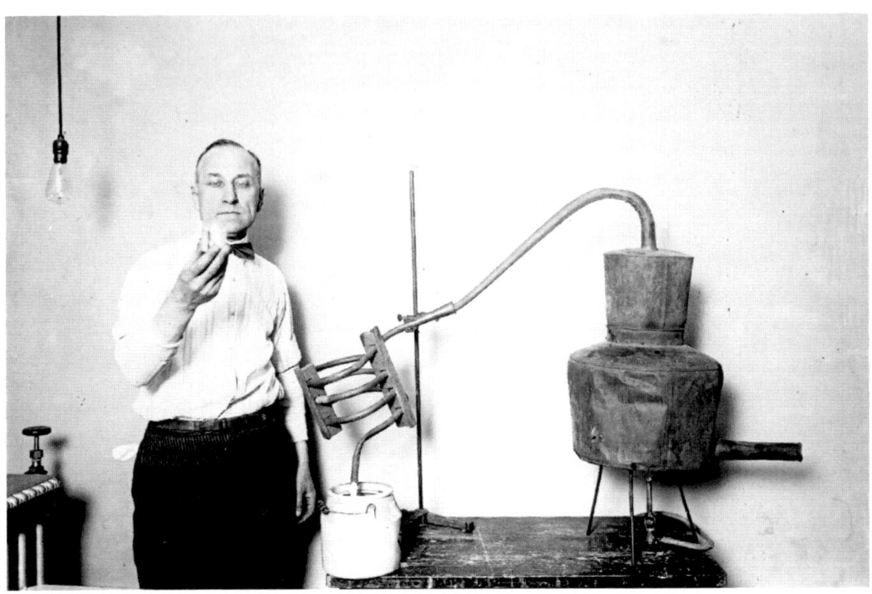

Government chemist tests alcohol content from a seized still. *Library of Congress.*

were able to obtain smell warrants, enabling them to search a building if they could smell mash.

Pittsburgh police lieutenant Eliss Wintzell had a nose for booze. He would leave his station house, stand outside and take a deep breath of air. He could not only smell the mash but also track the odor to a specific location. He once followed his nose to an address that resulted in the arrest of five men and the seizure of a ten-gallon still in the basement, five barrels of whiskey and two barrels of moonshine.

Bootleggers also sold "third rail" whiskey that was aged for an hour after distilling. Bartenders at speakeasies kept a pint of whiskey in their back pockets, so when a customer came in for a taste, the bartender would pour a shot and tell the patron to "get it down quick. Hurry up," while keeping an eye on the door. If agents raided the place, the bartender couldn't be arrested for violating the Volstead Act because he was carrying the liquor on his person, which wasn't illegal.

Pennsylvania governor Gifford Pinchot ordered saloons closed and forced bars to remove signs and other fixtures that would prevent agents from peering inside. Pinchot was a forester by training and served as chief of the U.S. Forest Service under Teddy Roosevelt. He studied forestry in Germany as a young man and was appalled by the drinking habits of Germans.

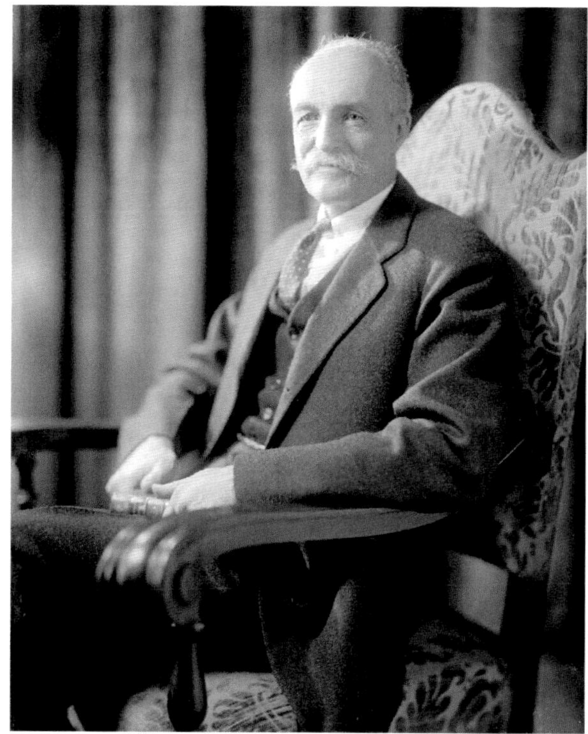

Governor Gifford Pinchot was an ardent dry. Even his speeches were dry, said a critic. *Library of Congress.*

"I want to put the padlocks on the doors of every saloon in the state," said Pinchot, an ardent dry, in an address to state lawmakers reported in the *Pittsburgh Press*. "The staples already have been driven and the padlocks are ready and it will not be long before the job will be done and the saloons closed for good."

Pittsburgh officials mocked Pinchot's stand on booze, said Paul B. Beers, a historian of Pennsylvania politics, in his book *Pennsylvania Politics: A Tolerable Accommodation*. "He is just as dry in a wet city when he is campaigning as he is in a dry county district," said future Pittsburgh mayor David Lawrence. "There's not a drop of moisture in any of his speeches."

Bold talk by Pinchot was not enough to stem the flow of booze into Pittsburgh and the region. Since 1912, hundreds of speakeasies, saloons and blind pigs had been operating in the city and Allegheny County that attracted working men who could not afford the high-priced drinks at licensed bars, restaurants and hotels.

A person had to be careful where he bought his whiskey and moonshine. Some of the moonshine could kill you in minutes. People were so desperate for a drink that they drank antifreeze from automobiles. Three people died after drinking antifreeze in a concoction known as an "antifreeze cocktail" at a drinking party on Herr's Island on the Allegheny River. Seven people died in Pittsburgh in 1922 from drinking poisoned liquor.

Others died after going blind from drinking wood alcohol. A twenty-year-old man went blind and an eight-year-old boy died after drinking wood alcohol in 1924. Four years later, a young married couple died after drinking wintergreen coloring to toast the New Year. Some people died of physical injuries after falling and fracturing their skulls while intoxicated. A widow died within eight months after spending her late husband's $1,000 life insurance policy on moonshine. Andrew Levandosky drank poisoned bootleg alcohol and then went on a shooting rampage, killing his wife and trying to kill his daughter before shooting himself. Authorities said Levandosky went wild from drinking the poisoned booze.

Deaths nationwide from alcohol poisoning were six hundred times higher in 1930 than in 1920, according to insurance company records. An estimated 5,000 people per month died from alcohol. The Prudential Life Insurance Company reported 1,000 deaths annually from alcohol poisoning at the start of Prohibition. That number would rise to 5,000 as Prohibition continued. In Pennsylvania, alcohol-related deaths averaged 25 per year until peaking at 137 in 1919.

Hucksters tried to dupe the public with snake oil medicines, such as Asprinol, which ads claimed was a remedy for the flu and colds. "Better Than Whiskey—Why?" read an ad. The makers claimed Asprinol contained 10 percent alcohol along with the "latest scientific remedies" that would provide "immediate relief" and a "quick warm-up." The government ordered the product off the market because the drug contained more than 15 percent alcohol, along with sodium salicylate; camphor, to give it a medicinal taste; the skin of coffee beans; and belladonna, which is a toxic substance from tomato plants that can cause delirium and hallucinations.

Another remedy touted for boosting energy, curing insomnia and improving bowel movements was Todd's Tonic, which was a medicinal-tasting drink that ads touted as tasting "just like wine"—because that's what the tonic contained.

Some companies were allowed to produce alcohol for industrial use in solvents and paints but were required to denature the alcohol by adding extra methyl alcohol or wood alcohol to make it undrinkable. Bootleggers hired chemists to remove the poisons by using a formula known as 39b, which was used to make perfume and cosmetics. The government countered the practice by adding kerosene and benzene.

Denatured alcohol was very much in demand. When bootleggers got ahold of shipments of denatured alcohol, they chemically removed the poisons so it could be distilled into liquor. Agents seized eight railroad cars filled with denatured alcohol in Pittsburgh's railyards in 1927 that had been shipped from New York to Pittsburgh under a false name and listed as creosote.

Methyl alcohol, known as "white mule," didn't immediately kill a person. It gave a drinker the familiar buzz that whiskey or a cocktail would but only for a short period of time. After drinking methyl alcohol, a person would first get a headache, followed by dizziness, nausea, confusion and the overwhelming need to sleep. As little as two teaspoons could kill a child while a quarter cup could cause blindness in an adult before inducing a coma and death. The liver has a difficult time breaking down wood alcohol, making it more poisonous. When a person drinks moonshine, the enzymes in the liver break down methyl alcohol, creating formic acid. Ethyl alcohol dissolves into acetic acid, which is harmless.

Beer arrived in Pittsburgh smuggled from Detroit via truck, train or river barges. There was "alley beer," so called because it was loaded into trucks from secret breweries where the trucks were parked in alleys so they wouldn't attract the attention of police. There was "near beer" and "diverted beer," which didn't have the alcohol removed, and home-brew.

The liquor that wasn't imported was made locally by "cookers," who operated in kitchens, cellars, warehouses and apartments. Large-scale bootleggers built elaborate stills hidden in warehouses, farms and abandoned factories. There were so many stills brewing and distilling in Pittsburgh that the air above the city smelled of mash. Home-brewing could be dangerous if you didn't know what you were doing. In 1926, a still exploded in the house of a city police detective when it overheated. Others were killed and badly burned when stills exploded. Newspapers advertised classes on how to make beer at home. For fifty dollars, a person could take a two-week course in home-brewing.

Cookers were paid \$1.50 a gallon, which sold for \$4.00. Out of that amount, \$2.50 went to pay off cops and politicians. "It bought Cadillacs and blondes for city and county officials and cops," wrote Ray Sprigle, a Pulitzer Prize–winning journalist for the *Pittsburgh Post-Gazette*.

Yeast and sugar were key ingredients in making booze and were in great demand, as were vanilla extract, flavoring ingredients, bottles, labels and caps.

Treasury secretary Andrew Mellon assigned a series of administrators to oversee the Pittsburgh region, but they were frustrated in attempts to enforce the Volstead Act because of indifference from Mellon and his underlings, as well as Pittsburgh police and city officials, who were opposed to Prohibition.

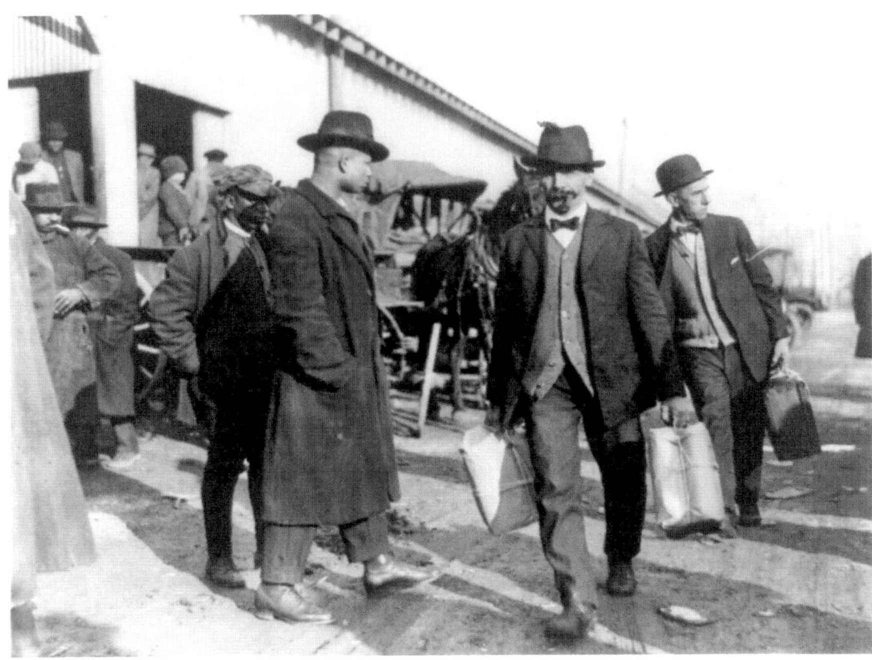

Federal agents carry off confiscated moonshine after a raid. *Library of Congress.*

The first Prohibition administrator in Pittsburgh was J.W. Connors, who bragged that within a year the city would look like a desert. "We feel assured before another anniversary of the Prohibition law is observed, Pittsburgh and western Pennsylvania will take on the semblance of the Sahara," Connor said.

Police, bootleggers and speakeasy operators worked hand in hand. Policemen were stationed outside speakeasies to control crowds. They had no intention of aiding federal agents during raids. Agents raided a huge brewery, seizing air compressors, twenty-two five-hundred-gallon stills and sixteen barrels of beer that were guarded by Pittsburgh police officers. "What's goin' on?" demanded a city cop. "We're supposed to be guardin' this thing," reported the *Pittsburgh Press*. During another raid, Pittsburgh cops showed up and got into a brawl with the agents.

"Let the Prohibition enforcement authorities make the raids and enforce the prohibition laws if they have any evidence," said Pittsburgh Public Safety director James Clark in response to complaints about the lack of cooperation with federal agents in the *Pittsburgh Press*. "Nothing would please me better. That is what prohibition agents are for."

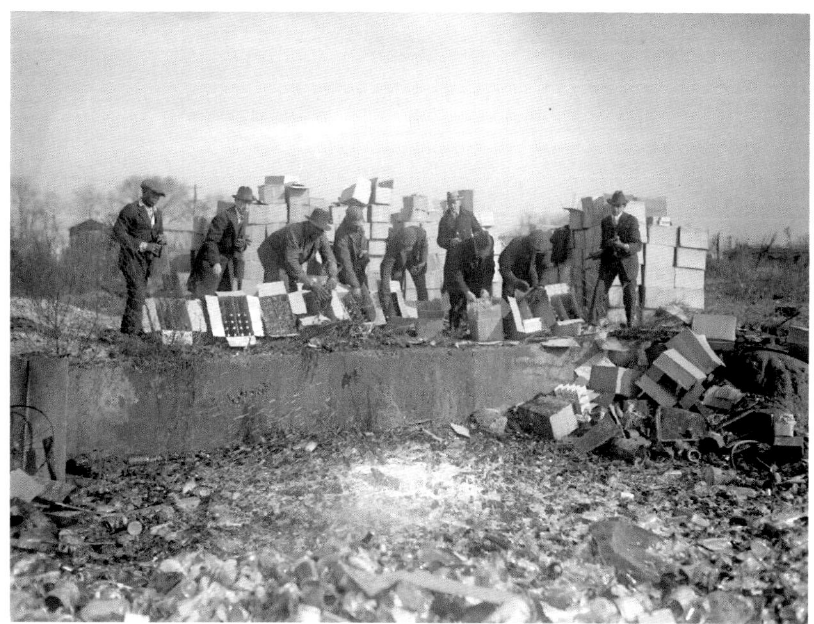

Agents dispose of seized illegal liquor. *Library of Congress.*

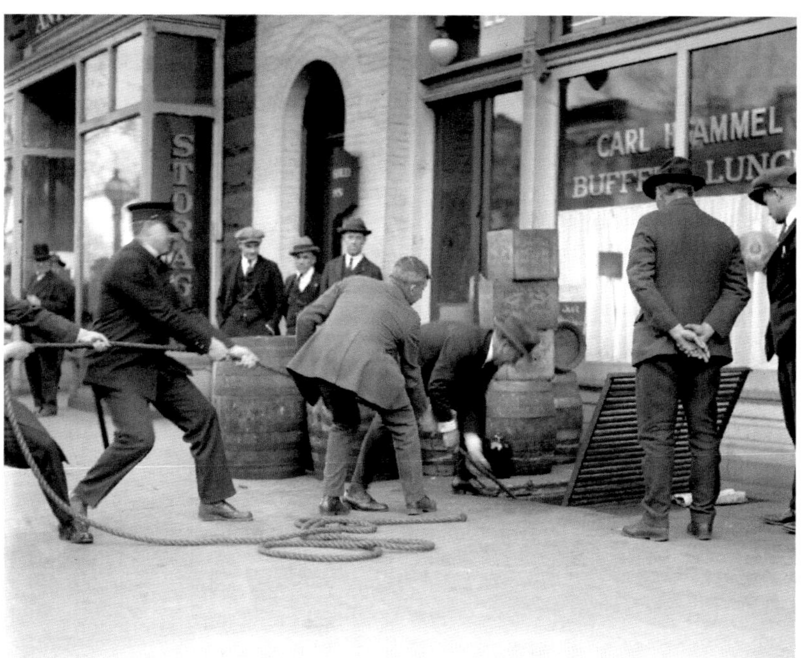

"Let the federal men raid," said Pittsburgh police, who often were in cahoots with bootleggers and refused to enforce the law. In this image, agents raid a speakeasy. *Library of Congress.*

Pittsburgh newspapers criticized Clark for his attitude. The public expected the police to conduct "as many raids as necessary and against speakeasies as well as against gambling or other dens," read an editorial in the *Pittsburgh Post-Gazette*. "No matter what a public officer may think of prohibition or any law, it is not his business to repeal them as long as they remain on the books."

After a truckload of liquor was seized by agents, the shipment was stored at a Pittsburgh police station and then promptly disappeared. The liquor was recovered, but officials never reconciled the exact amount that was missing because none of the tally sheets matched the original.

Agents were hamstrung by red tape in carrying out the law. They could not conduct raids after sundown, when most of the liquor law violations occurred. Agents had to purchase liquor and then obtain an affidavit from a federal magistrate before the magistrate would issue a search warrant. Then agents had to stage the raid and seize the booze, but afterward, they had to return to court to obtain an arrest warrant. Once the warrant was issued, a U.S. marshal would make the arrest. By the time the violator appeared in court, his bail would be waiting for his release. The bootlegger would have made enough money between the time of his release and trial to pay a fine.

The next administrator to run into judicial red tape was John Enciosis, who, in 1921, had earned a reputation in California for cleaning up dope dens. He, too, felt frustrated by a lack of support from his bosses. "This is one place in the county as far as I know where a Prohibition agent can't arrest a man seen violating the law," he said. "It is a question of law interpretation and it hinders us tremendously in our work." Enciosis was replaced because of his criticism of the federal judiciary in Pittsburgh.

His replacement, Edgar Ray, resigned in frustration, charging the federal government never had any intention of enforcing the law. "I do not care to be identified with the work any longer. It is my opinion this is the biggest swindle ever perpetrated in this country," reported the *Gazette Times*.

Maurice Campbell, who served for a time as national administrator of Prohibition under Treasury secretary Andrew Mellon, said Mellon was livid after Campbell's agents raided the Ritz-Carlton Hotel in New York City, a place where Mellon stayed when he was in New York. Agents also raided a speakeasy in a building Mellon owned in Pittsburgh, confiscating 1,400 bottles of beer, 100 cases of beer, 25 pints of whiskey, 3 cases of malt and 20 cases of gin.

"My experience has been that Prohibition enforcement is honey combed with political insincerity and corruption radiating from Washington to every state, city and town in the United States," said Campbell in a series of nationally syndicated stories that was reprinted in the *Pittsburgh Press*. Corruption, Campbell added, "radiated from Washington."

Campbell pointed out that when an official within his department refused to issue a permit for the National Grain Yeast Company to sell the commodity, National Grain hired attorney David E.K. Bruce, the son-in-law of Secretary Mellon, to plead its case. The official was transferred and the permit granted, Campbell said.

Campbell also charged that he was ordered by his superiors to ease up on enforcement by calling off raids in New York so the Republican Party could secure dry votes. He said Andrew Mellon personally reviewed the order and made changes in the document in his own handwriting. He also said Treasury officials ordered agents to stop putting breweries under surveillance.

Then Campbell said he was offered $250,000 in bribes to ease up on the regulations governing sacramental wine by allowing rabbis to supervise the distribution. He said he also was offered the opportunity to open his own advertising agency. Campbell's wife was an actress and was offered a role in a Broadway play if she would use her influence on her husband to help out a certain distillery.

John D. Pennington, a former navy commander, was the most aggressive administrator assigned to Pittsburgh. Pennington grew up on a potato farm and ran away from home at sixteen to join the navy. He rose in the ranks from seaman to commander and fought in the Spanish-American War, the Boxer Rebellion and World War I.

He conducted more than fifteen thousand raids between July 1926 and April 1930. He arrested over seventeen thousand violators, closed more than 3,200 distilleries and destroyed 4,500 stills. His agents seized 3.4 million gallons of mash, 8,000 gallons of moonshine and 113,000 gallons of alcohol. He reduced the number of speakeasies from 522 to 9. That record was too much for Pittsburgh politicians, whose graft and political survival was tied to liquor production. After exerting political pressure on Mellon, Pennington was reassigned to Philadelphia.

In a farewell speech before he went east, Pennington said the city officials protected bootleggers "up to the point of murder." He charged there was an "unholy alliance between corrupt politics and the underworld fosters our present lawlessness. There is entirely too much 'trading' and 'fixing' being engaged in by district attorneys and other prosecuting officers, puny fines and sentences utterly fail as a deterrent to crime and judges responsible are miserably negligent to their duty to properly protect and safeguard society."

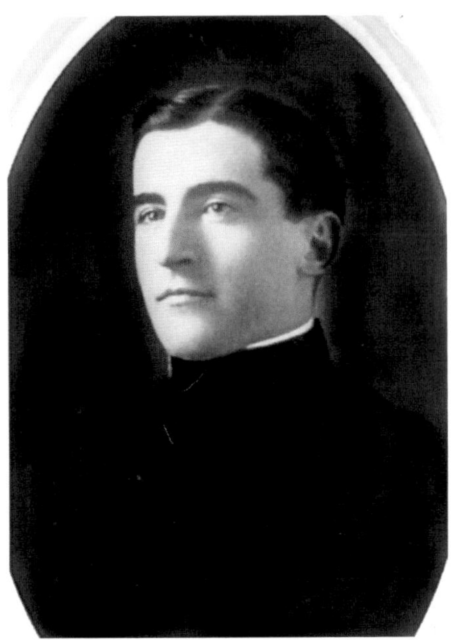

The aggressive John D. Pennington, Pittsburgh Prohibition administrator, as a naval officer. *Archives Service Center, University of Pittsburgh.*

"It is the fix or official, the corrupt politician, the corrupt judge on the bench, the corrupt prosecutor in office of public trust who deserves condemnation for a reign of lawlessness which should have been intolerable long ago," said Pennington.

He tried to foster better cooperation between his agents, Pittsburgh police and the district attorney in Allegheny County, but the DA refused to prosecute liquor cases brought by Pennington's men. A near riot erupted at a Pittsburgh police station between Pennington's agents and city officers. "It was a fine spectacle of lawlessness for city policemen and officers of the United States government to the public," reported one newspaper.

Pennington's philosophy was not to go after the small-time bootleggers or consumers who carried hip flasks. Instead, he focused on the bootleggers who made the hooch and grew wealthy in the process. Pennington was lauded for his stance by a Pittsburgh newspaper, which criticized local police for not doing enough.

"City police would be more effective enforcing Prohibition if they wanted to. The extent to which the law is ignored and the viciousness which results, is appalling to decent people, to dregs and to those who abhor Prohibition but advocate temperance and tolerance," read an editorial in the *Pittsburgh Press* in 1928.

Pittsburgh cops drank in the speakeasies that they were supposed to raid and were protected by their superiors. Bootleggers paid police officials for protection and allowed these illegal establishments to operate across the street from a police station.

When Allegheny County judge Frank Patterson learned an exclusive speakeasy, Club Monaca, was operating in 1932 under the very noses of the police, he ordered police and constables to appear in court to explain why they hadn't raided the club. Patterson said the club had become a haunt for Pittsburgh's "better citizens," who gained entry through a back door after going through two steel doors. The judge launched investigations into politically protected speakeasies in five city wards. Patterson said in remarks published in the *Pittsburgh Press*:

> *Men are being slaughtered on the streets at high noon. Citizens are afraid to go abroad after dark. Banditry and revelry is on the streets of the city. I know it's not your fault but it is an outgrowth of trafficking between criminals and the law. Speakeasies and gambling houses are not so bad in themselves but they breed crime.*
>
> *These violations exist only through the bartering of the law offices with the operators of these places. Some powerful influence as strong as it is corrupt must be protecting these places.*

Police inspector James Hoey was replaced because he refused to grant a permit for the Monaca Club to operate. As soon as he was transferred, the club opened. One of the Monaca Club's owners was Tom Coyne, the brother of state senator James Coyne, a political power broker in the city. Patterson became indignant when police told him they had no idea that the place was a speakeasy. Patterson said the police and local constables were a "blind man's parade." The sounds of soft music mixed with the rattle of dice, the clink of ice in cocktail glasses and the whirl of the roulette wheel could be heard in the street. Troopers found a brewery in the basement and slot machines on the third floor.

Since Pittsburgh police wouldn't raid the club, Governor Pinchot ordered state police to investigate. Undercover troopers went to the club posing as fans from a Saturday football game between Washington & Jefferson College and Duquesne University. After buying drinks, they signaled to their confederates outside to begin the raid where two hundred patrons were drinking and gambling. One employee joked, according to the *Pittsburgh Press*, "Gee, a guy can't earn an honest living even in these times."

The club was known locally as the "three Toms's Club" because it was owned by Tom Coyne, Tom Goslin and Tom Dolin, a former speakeasy owner. Goslin was a racketeer and former boxer. The men were tried, convicted and sentenced to six months in jail each only after a plot to "fix" the jury in the first trial was uncovered, forcing the judge to declare a mistrial.

The raids by state police had the desired effect. Bootleggers were on edge. One rumor circulating was that three convicted bootleggers serving time in the federal prison in Atlanta were coming back to Pittsburgh to "squawk" on their cohorts and implicate powerful political figures in the liquor trade.

Police handled bootleggers with kid gloves even before Prohibition. The president of the Pittsburgh City Council in 1916 berated the police in the *Gazette Times* for allowing crime to exist in certain parts of the city. He said the Hill District was "wide open" with speakeasies and gambling dens. "There is a speakeasy at almost every door and that gambling is widespread," he said. "Either the police do not know their duty or they are not trying to perform it."

Mayor Charles Kline turned graft into an efficient business while turning a blind eye to the daily violence. During his fifty-one months in office, there were more than one hundred murders. Police corruption was well organized during Kline's administration. Kline, who would be convicted of malfeasance in office and sentenced to prison, divided the city into zones and limited the amount of graft police officials could accept to $30,000 a year.

The *Pittsburgh Post-Gazette* waged a campaign against vice and the Kline administration's failure to clean up the city by publishing photos of Prohibition dives on the Northside along with white arrows showing the entrance to the joints. They also published the names of the bootleggers who ran the speakeasies and those of the police officials who protected them.

It was hard for poorly paid police officers to shun the cash that was spread around during Prohibition. To become a cop, an individual had to know someone with the political clout. Once hired, they had to buy their own uniforms, guns, ammunition, badges and nightsticks. Many cops were illiterate or had no formal education. Most officers worked as substitutes before being hired full time, so paychecks were few and far between.

Officers had to be politically active if they wanted to keep their jobs. Herman Stubenrauch had been fired from the force several times for beating people, trying to rob a saloon and threatening to kill a superior officer. He was fired as a Prohibition agent because he was corrupt and once shot up a car because he thought the driver "looked suspicious." Each time, Stubenrauch found a way to return to the police department because of his political connections.

When a U.S. Senate Committee was investigating the finances of Senator William Vare in the 1926 campaign, they subpoenaed Pittsburgh police superintendent Peter Walsh, who was accused of ordering his officers to wear campaign buttons supporting the candidacies of Senator George W. Pepper for reelection and John S. Fisher for governor. He also instructed patrolmen to provide him with a list of election returns showing the vote count for each candidate. Vare defeated Pepper and Fisher won the nomination for governor. The senators were investigating a $3 million slush fund in the election campaign that was generously supported by the owners of speakeasies and saloons.

Walsh was one of the most corrupt police officers in Pittsburgh and was known as the "czar" because of the power he wielded. Ministers criticized Walsh for his "shameless toleration of vice and racketeering." Walsh joined the police department in 1898. He was promoted to lieutenant in 1903 and then captain and inspector. He became superintendent in 1914. Walsh served under Mayor Charles Kline and was "an important cog in the wrecked political machine" of Kline's administration. He was indicted for corruption in 1928 but escaped conviction.

During his testimony, Walsh told the committee Pittsburgh had "no dives" and that since he wasn't a drinking man, he didn't know the difference between a saloon and a club. When warrants were issued for five suspects accused of running a $300,000 liquor operation, police allowed them to remain free until they chose to surrender. Police rode shotgun on beer trucks that rumbled through the city at night making deliveries to prevent hijacking. Sometimes, Pittsburgh cops peppered federal agents with buckshot after raids, and a cop once assaulted a federal agent with a nightstick.

A federal grand jury in Pittsburgh in 1928 indicted 167 individuals for conspiracy to violate the Volstead Act. The defendants included members of Mayor Kline's administration, police magistrates, Superintendent Walsh, three police inspectors, a dozen lieutenants, four patrolmen, two state legislators and five GOP ward chairmen. State lawmaker Samuel Grenet, owner the Fort Pitt Brewing Company, was accused of allowing his brewery to clandestinely brew beer and distill whiskey. Legislator Luke Sullivan was the brother of U.S congressman P.J. Sullivan of Pittsburgh. Bail for the defendants totaled $835,000.

The indictment said the police ruled bootleggers with an "iron hand" and ordered, sold, delivered and protected liquor shipments to speakeasies and clubs in the North and South Sides, the Strip District, East End and downtown neighborhoods. Charges also alleged police officials were in cahoots with members of Pittsburgh's underworld. On the day he was to testify, a key grand jury witness was shot and wounded.

The government alleged police officials acted as "fixers" and "go-betweens" for the elected officials and bootleggers and gamblers. The grand jury also subpoenaed the financial records of the defendants from forty-nine banks to trace the money. Two of the defendants, Stanley and John Orie, whose real last name was "Orzechowski," went to prison for income tax evasion. Orie, a police magistrate, failed to declare nearly $119,000 in income from bribes. He served 366 days in a federal prison. Stanley Orie served six months for evading taxes on nearly $75,000 in hidden income.

The two-year investigation by the federal government was a failure. Charges eventually were dropped against most of the defendants for a lack of evidence. Although Superintendent Walsh was acquitted, he was fired by Mayor John Herron for his "shameless toleration of vice and racketeering." Federal prosecutors subpoenaed the financial records of the officials in an effort to trace the money they earned from bootlegging.

During the course of the investigation, prosecutors subpoenaed Harry Dapper, the vice-president of the Fort Pitt Brewing Company, because a grand jury was investigating the mysterious death of Dapper's son, Dr. Harry Dapper, a twenty-seven-year-old physician. Dr. Dapper was murdered while responding to a request from a man who said his wife was pregnant and about to deliver a baby. The senior Dapper drove his son to the appointment, which was a ruse. Once there, they were beaten, and his son was shot.

Investigators suspected that the killing may have been linked to bootleggers since the elder Dapper worked for brewer Samuel Grenet, who was facing trial for violating the Volstead Act for adding alcohol to "near beer." Two men confessed to the crime but were never charged with the killing. One was serving a prison sentence in Illinois and later repudiated his confession. The confession of the second man was in doubt when the doctor's father could not identify him as one of the attackers. The grand jury also reviewed large deposits made by a woman who refused to answer questions about the money and was held in contempt. Young Dapper's killer never was found.

Federal agents stumbled on several police officers helping bootleggers unload a whiskey truck in McKees Rocks, which is located across the Ohio River from Pittsburgh. The bootleggers fled, but the agents arrested a police captain, a lieutenant and several patrolmen as they were unloading cases of beer that had been injected with alcohol and were destined for McKees Rocks saloons.

Pittsburgh policemen and local officers weren't the only ones susceptible to bribery. A number of current and former Prohibition agents were caught up in scandal. Saul Grill, a noted undercover Treasury agent, was sent to Pittsburgh to ferret out corruption. He discovered some agents accepted bribes to protect bootlegging operations or to tip off bootleggers to raids. Grill said one agent accepted $500,000 in bribes. Grill himself accepted $33,000 in hush money when bootleggers delivered a stack of bills to his hotel room.

"It's almost impossible for a man to go into Pennsylvania to enforce the Prohibition law and come out clean," Grill said, in an interview in the *Philadelphia Evening Ledger*. "If he is not a crook when he goes in the chances are he'll become one."

Agents' badges became licenses to get rich. Nationwide, 42 agents were convicted of corruption. Another one was convicted for murder. Between 1920 and 1930, nearly 12,000 agents out of a force of nearly 18,000 were fired after being accused of wrongdoing in cases where the crimes couldn't be proved. Low pay was the main reason Prohibition agents took bribes. When the law went into effect, there were 1,520 agents on the job nationwide, earning a paltry $1,200 to $2,000 a year. A decade later, there were 2,836 agents earning between $2,300 and $2,800 a year. Pennsylvania couldn't afford to pay state enforcement agents, so the Woman's Christian Temperance Union paid their salaries.

Pittsburgh policemen had been protecting saloons for decades prior to Prohibition. George H. Waggoner, chief of Allegheny County detectives, was a city cop before joining the county detectives. He had investigated a Strip District organization known as the Bayardstown Hunting and Fishing Club, owned by city councilman Bernard Kenna, that Waggoner charged was a speakeasy. Waggoner was brought up before the police trial board, and the investigation into the club was ended. Waggoner left the force, claiming the investigation was a "whitewash."

There were separate systems of justice for bootleggers and the average citizen. A police magistrate allowed a major bootlegger to walk out of court with a $100 fine while he held for trial a mother of thirteen children who operated a small home still to earn money to support her kids. The mother pleaded for mercy.

"Can't you be lenient with me?" she pleaded. "If you had 20 children it wouldn't matter," replied the magistrate in a *Pittsburgh Press* story.

The police department was controlled by politics. The mayor held sway over the city, but police magistrates had gun-toting constables who had the same powers of arrest as police officers. The mayor often was at odds with the police magistrates, who ran their own protection rackets and often came into conflict with police over police-protected speakeasies and bootlegging operations.

In 1928, the foundation of Pittsburgh's system of graft and corruption was shaken to the core when Magistrate John Verona, a big, tough-talking Italian, ex-Prohibition agent and former bootlegger, decided he had tired of city policemen raiding speakeasies in his jurisdiction, especially those under his protection.

Verona was at political odds with another ex-bootlegger, John Engelsberg, for political control of the volatile and important Third Ward in the Hill District. During the 1930 general election, the two sides each proposed a slate of election judges that was packed with the names of convicted bootleggers and gamblers. Control of elected office was crucial in protecting the speakeasies and gambling dens that proliferated in the Hill District.

Verona and Engelsberg accused each other's nominees of being criminals. Engelsberg charged that one of Verona's handpicked nominees was "conducting a still and is a known bootlegger." Verona responded that an Engelsberg candidate ran a speakeasy "which was later blown up" by a bomb.

Verona also was at odds with Mayor Charles Kline and his surrogate, police inspector Hoey, who led raids in Verona's Third Ward in the Hill District. Hoey was an appointee of Senator James Coyne, another longtime Verona nemesis. In 1933, Verona was subpoenaed to testify before a federal grand jury investigating election fraud. When Verona appeared, he refused to answer any of the panel's questions, invoking the Fifth Amendment against self-incrimination. Afterward, he attacked Coyne for instigating the investigation.

As an alderman, it was Verona's responsibility to guard the election returns. Instead of having the results of the voting returned to his office, he had them diverted to a private club where they were counted, leading to allegations that the votes were mishandled and Verona blaming Coyne for alerting the federal authorities.

The Hill District and Strip District were on the verge of warfare between the magistrates and police in 1928. Both sides often fought each other. If a constable discovered that speakeasy owners were not buying beer from favored bootleggers, they would raid and arrest the saloonkeepers. If the targets of the raid happened to be protected by the mayor, city detectives would raid a spot protected by the police magistrates.

Since Verona also was a police magistrate, he had a small army of constables working for him to conduct his own raids on police-protected speakeasies. In 1928, Pittsburgh cops raided a speakeasy in the Hill District and nabbed twenty-two politicians, including Verona. Verona told the arresting officers his name was "Mike O'Brien," but the police knew Verona by sight.

Verona soon retaliated against Hoey by sending constables to arrest him for assault. Verona charged that Hoey browbeat and physically assaulted the men and women he arrested. The constables arrived at the Central Police Station as Hoey was leaving and tried to arrest him. A gunfight broke out. To avoid arrest, Hoey locked himself in a jail cell at the police station.

When Pittsburgh detectives, armed with a search warrant, raided a Verona-protected speakeasy, he had the detectives arrested. He refused to allow them to post bond and forced them to spend a night in jail.

Mayor Kline asked Verona to resign. Verona refused, so Kline fired him as magistrate. Verona retaliated by accusing Kline and police of protecting bootleggers, gambling clubs and slot machine operators. "I'll stand by the charges," Verona said in the *Pittsburgh Press*. "I'll not back down." Hoey accused Verona of using his constables to protect certain vice operations in his ward. Verona was subpoenaed to repeat his charges before an Allegheny County Grand Jury that had been empaneled to investigate the allegations, but no one ever was indicted.

Political control of the Hill District was vital to the survival of vice lords. Reelection for a candidate meant they could continue to control bootlegging, gambling and prostitution. The slate of candidates in the 1930 election contained the names of convicted bootleggers, number operators, slot machine owners and bawdy house madams.

Verona remained a man of political influence until 1937, when he dropped dead of a heart attack in the middle of a brawl at the Benjamin Harrison Literary Club. Verona's funeral was befitting a gangster who had been "put on the spot" by gunmen. More than ten thousand people stood outside the Catholic church where Verona's funeral was held.

Governor Pinchot blamed Secretary Mellon for "being the chief obstacle to Prohibition enforcement" and refusing to carry out the duties of his office. Pinchot and Mellon hated each other. During the worst days of the Great Depression, Pinchot had asked Mellon to loan Pennsylvania $35 million, but Mellon refused. The GOP in Pennsylvania was factionalized, with Pinchot representing the progressive wing while Mellon controlled the party through extensive patronage and his fortune.

Pinchot said Mellon's lack of interest in enforcing the law stemmed from the fact that he owned the Old Overholt Distillery in neighboring Westmoreland County, which Mellon purchased from Henry Clay Frick for $25,000 and later sold for $4.5 million. Pinchot also spread the rumor that Mellon was smuggling whiskey in empty Gulf oil barrels and selling the booze at Gulf gas stations. Pinchot's feud with Mellon was detailed in a fawning biography of Mellon by Philip H. Love, *Andrew W. Mellon, the Man and His Work.*

"Secretary Mellon, for the better part of a generation, was a whiskey distributor and only within the last couple of weeks divested of his interest in million dollars' worth of whiskey and has chosen to enforcement the law

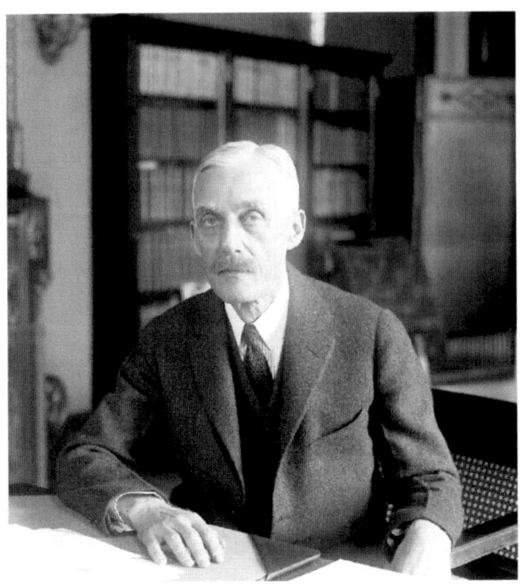

Treasury secretary Andrew Mellon of Pittsburgh owned a distillery but claimed little knowledge of its operations. *Library of Congress.*

and accept responsibility for enforcing the law," Pinchot charged. "Secretary Mellon has for four years had the power and the money and by driving politics out of the enforcement service he could at any time have had the men."

Mellon was asked about his ownership of Old Overholt by a Senate committee: "Was it your intention to engage in that business? If not, why was that distillery purchased?"

Mellon raised his arm to slide back his coat sleeve. "I have nothing up my sleeve," he replied.

He said he invested in the distillery a few years before Prohibition was enacted. "Since that time I have had no concern or connection with the property or business. I do not know how many gallons of liquor were held at the time when the 18th Amendment and Volstead Act became effective. In fact, I have never known."

Mellon was lying. In 1925, as Treasury secretary, he issued a government permit to the distillery so his company could sell medicinal whiskey from its idle stock and would have known how much the company was planning to sell. Prohibition agents also raided a downtown Pittsburgh building owned by Mellon that contained a large supply of whiskey, wine and beer, adding to the public's lack of confidence in Mellon as an enforcer of the law.

Another piece of evidence that showed Mellon wasn't entirely truthful surfaced in 1934, when Mellon sued the IRS, claiming the government imposed the same taxes twice on two companies—A. Overholt & Company and West Overton Distilling Company—and was seeking a refund of $550,000. Mellon's attorneys argued no liquor was distilled between 1917 and 1920, but the companies had sixty thousand barrels in their inventories by 1920.

Mellon was unable to escape criticism even from his own party. Senator Smith W. Brookhart of Iowa complained in an article in the *Pittsburgh Press* that Mellon's Wall Street cronies had invited him to a party in 1926 where whiskey flasks were handed to senators as gifts. "Who is to blame? I'll tell you. I'm not after the little fellows. The man who is to blame is Andrew Mellon."

The Board of Temperance, Prohibition and Public Morals of the Methodist Episcopal Church also had little faith in Mellon, wrote Lisa McGirr, a Harvard professor and author of *The War on Alcohol: The Rise of the American State*. "Neither by caution not by inclination is he fit for that responsibility," reported the board.

Pittsburgh and western Pennsylvania was filled with breweries and distilleries. The city had three major breweries: Fort Pitt, Duquesne and the Independent Brewing Company. Fort Pitt opened in 1908 and remained open during Prohibition by producing a line of nonalcoholic beverages even though more than 60 percent of its sales were to saloons before the law went into effect.

The Duquesne Brewing Company prospered after Prohibition, producing 337,000 barrels in 1937. Smaller operations were located in Carnegie, McKees Rock and McKeesport in Allegheny County. Regional breweries dotted western Pennsylvania. The Benedictine monks at St. Vincent Archabbey and Seminary made beer from the grains they grew on farmland. They built a small brewery and began selling the product locally until Prohibition forced its closing in 1919. There also were small breweries in adjoining counties. Latrobe and Monessen in Westmoreland County had breweries.

Stoney's Beer was made in Smithton in Westmoreland County. The brewery was founded by W.B. Jones Jr., whose nickname was "Stoney." The beer got its name when people began asking for beer made by Stoney. Jones's granddaughter is actress Shirley Jones.

Old Overholt in West Overton produced Old Farm Pure Rye, which reportedly was the favorite drink of gambler and gunfighter Doc Holliday. In 1800, Henry Overholt arrived in the region. He hacked out a farm and gristmill from the forest and began growing rye.

His son, Abraham, who was the grandfather of industrialist Henry Clay Frick, persuaded his father in 1810 to build a distillery. Even though they were Mennonites and frowned on whiskey distilling, the Overholts produced two hundred gallons of rye a day, marketing the whiskey as "Old Farm Rye" and later "Old Overholt."

5
The Great Wet Way

Downtown Pittsburgh was known as the "Great Wet Way" making the city the "drinkingest town in the west," according to a story in the *Literary Guild*, during Prohibition because of the amount of illegal booze that found its way into speakeasies.

"We've got Prohibition in Pittsburgh only on paper," said a Treasury Department official in the same story.

The Volstead Act failed to make a dent in the flow of liquor in Pittsburgh, which was described as "wet enough for rubber boots" and western Pennsylvania as the "wettest spot in the nation," reported the magazine.

Clandestine breweries made the city "one of the wettest points on the compass," according to a Treasury Department official testifying before a U.S. Senate committee

Politicians took advantage of their ties to bootleggers. When city officials held a junket on the Ohio River for a group of politically connected friends, the alcohol and cigars were provided by bootleggers. Bootleggers were asked—or rather ordered—to provide "refreshments" for the soiree and were "expected not to send any bills," which amounted to $25,000, as a small price for protection.

Liquor smuggling in Pittsburgh was well organized. A group of local politicians used a closed brewery in eastern Pennsylvania to brew and ship beer to Pittsburgh. They divided the city into zones. Each zone had a manager to handle sales. Saloons and speakeasies purchased their supplies directly from a zone manager who arranged for deliveries. Business boomed and bootleggers grew rich because it only cost bootleggers thirty-seven cents to make a gallon of beer that they sold for three dollars.

Thieves broke into railroad cars, searching for liquor stashed in the baggage of passengers. "The whiskey hunter only wants the liquid," William J. Flynn, chief of the U.S. Secret Service, told the *Gazette Times*. The number of thefts was so great that the Pennsylvania Railroad stopped serving drinks in its dining cars. Smugglers also hid liquor on trains to sneak alcohol into Pittsburgh.

Bootleggers found other ways to get around the ban on liquor. They built large stills hidden in abandoned buildings. Agents found one still that was used to scald the hides of pigs and contained the bodies of rats. People brewed beer in their homes in what were known as "kitchen stills." Walk by a neighbor's house, and you could smell mash wafting in the air.

"They always were blowing up," said a Northside resident as part of the oral history collection at the Carnegie in Pittsburgh. "You heard—just like a shot—and we would all laugh about it."

For some, it was no laughing matter. Two people in Pittsburgh were killed and three others burned in 1927 when a still exploded in their house.

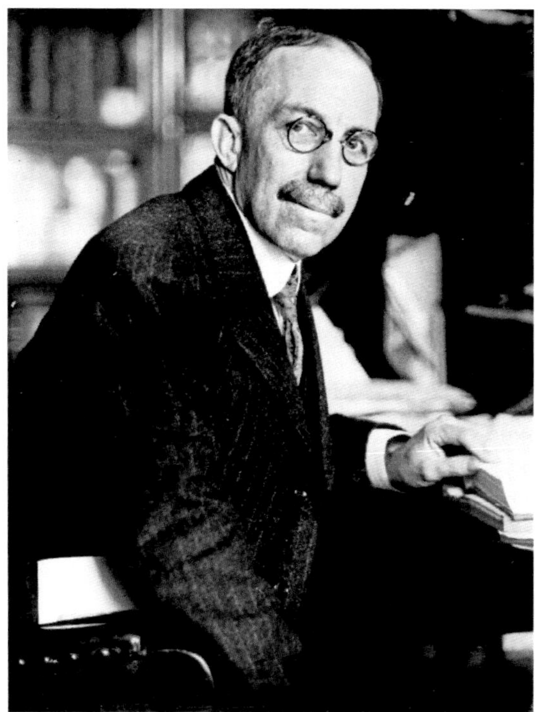

The powerful Wayne Wheeler, head of the Anti-Saloon League. *Library of Congress.*

Explosions were caused by a buildup of alcohol vapors. When the fumes reached seventy-two degrees, they sought room to expand. Many home-based stills weren't properly vented, which allowed the vapors to accumulate at dangerous levels.

There were nine breweries at one time on the North Side of Pittsburgh that served as a food source for hungry families during the Depression. Some breweries were allowed to remain open to process grains for cereals. Mothers would send their children to the breweries carrying small tin buckets so the kids could scoop up the hot, steaming mash. They came out in large cakes, which the brewers sold to farmers for animal feed. "Mother made a gruel from the mash and flavored it with molasses," said one interviewee from the Pittsburgh Oral Histories collection at the Carnegie Library.

"It was good mash," said the woman who remembered eating the gruel as a child, according to the oral history account. "It was barley and oats and it was all good grain. There was enough to feed five children."

The Great Depression brought industry in Pittsburgh to its collective knees by 1932. Thousands were jobless, and thousands more were starving. Every day, hundreds of men lined up at soup kitchens around Pittsburgh. Shantytowns housing the homeless began to appear on the urban landscape. The failing economy drove men to sell booze to support their families.

A steward at a Pittsburgh club was fined $100 by a federal judge for selling liquor because he needed money to feed his family. One bootlegger, who could not speak or hear, turned to bootlegging to support his wife, seven children and eighty-eight-year-old mother-in-law. Another man became a bootlegger after he broke his leg and could no longer work. A Pittsburgh newspaper lamented the problems that Prohibition had wrought on the working class.

"We can conceive of men so desperate for money to feed their families that they would be glad to get a job in a club where liquor is for sale," read an editorial in the *Pittsburgh Press*. "If liquor was being sold under government regulation, such men would have legitimate jobs. So speed the day when America shall be free of the curse of the Eighteenth Amendment and all the evils it has borne."

Bootlegging remained the only thriving industry in the Pittsburgh region, generating millions of dollars that was spent paying off cops and politicians. The profits from bootlegging produced more money than Pittsburgh, Allegheny County and Pennsylvania combined could generate to pay for relief efforts.

Pittsburgh during Prohibition was an overpopulated city of over 700,000. The Allegheny, Monongahela and Ohio Rivers were filled with slag from the region's steel mills, and the streets were littered with garbage. The city's once smog-filled skies from the steel industry were now clear because the mills no longer were operating at full capacity.

City streets were clogged with traffic. By the late 1920s, there were more than 115,000 cars crossed city streets each day. That was 390 miles of vehicles in a city with only 12 miles of streets. There were only eighty hospital beds available in the entire city. Working-class neighborhoods developed and soon were filled with saloons, taverns and brothels.

The city's elite were Scotch-Irish Presbyterians who ruled the cultural, social, economic and financial worlds and treated the lower classes as vassals. "The 'supreme crime' in Pittsburgh was not murder and the violation of liquor laws," but the "willful defiance of the little group of Scottish Presbyterians who regard themselves as having been elected by providence to be the city's masters and also are, in fact, the city's masters," wrote R.L. Duffus in "Is Pittsburgh Civilized? for *Harper's* in 1932.

Treasury secretary Mellon became the symbol of corruption. A magazine cartoon depicted a winged Mellon aloft in a red, smoky sky high above the belching steel mills while beneath him lie dilapidated shacks and silk-hatted bankers making payoffs to corrupt politicians.

Mellon and his clan were Scotch-Irish Presbyterians committed to temperance, although Mellon was not averse to having a drink. In colonial times, many Scotch-Irish farmers distilled whiskey, and presbytery meetings often began with a drink among the ministers and church elders. They became more adamant about temperance in the nineteenth and at the start of the twentieth century, using the pulpit to preach against the evils of alcohol. Churches expelled members who drank to excess or distilled liquor for profit.

The 1920s ushered in the Progressive Era of political reform and attention to social issues. The nation severed its ties to the nineteenth century, when daily life had been centered on the farm, family and church. For the first time, more Americans lived in the city than in rural areas. There also was a proliferation of consumer goods. More people could afford cars. Movies had sound. Drinking habits changed. Women began drinking in public.

The Nineteenth Amendment gave women the right to vote. Religious fundamentalism became the backbone of the anti-alcohol movement. A great migration of African Americans, driven from their homes in the South by the boll weevil, arrived in Pittsburgh to fill jobs in the mills and coal mines.

The Ku Klux Klan responded to this invasion by aligning itself for a time with the Anti-Saloon League and intimidating African Americans and immigrants who were overwhelmingly Catholic and heavy drinkers. The Klan was anti-black, anti-Semitic, anti-Catholic and anti-immigrant. Membership in the Klan reached fifteen thousand in Pittsburgh and had an estimated sixty thousand members in western Pennsylvania between 1923 and 1925. Famed lawyer Clarence Darrow charged the "mother and father of the Ku Klux Klan is the Anti-Saloon League," according to Harvard's McGirr, author of *The War on Alcohol.*

Prohibition also brought about the advent of tabloid journalism, with front-page stories about sensational crime and political corruption. Young women dressed as "flappers," flouting conventional behavior by drinking, smoking, wearing their hair in a bob and covering their faces with rouge so thick their parents believed their children were headed for hell. Young men emulated film star Rudolph Valentino by dressing as "sheiks," young men on the make. The style was made popular by the 1921 silent film *The Sheik.*

The clergy lamented this changing of social mores. Father James R. Cox, pastor of Old St. Patrick's Church in Pittsburgh's Strip District, a hellhole of alcohol and vice, warned that "alcohol fumes do not spread an aroma of love around them," according to one of Cox's Sunday radio sermons that was covered by the *Pittsburgh Press* and *Pittsburgh Post-Gazette.* Cox's Sunday sermons were broadcast over a Pittsburgh radio station and often were front-page news in Monday's editions. Cox warned that women who drank alcohol would end up with husbands who were "bottle mates" rather than "love mates": "Neither will women and men attracted by the fumes of alcohol be husbands and wives. They may be found in wedlock by the law or church but they are not man and wife. They are merely bottle mates. A hug, a kiss, a drink, and marriage remove a woman's inherent qualities and leave no thrill for the man, and when beauty and thrill is gone, life is not worth living."

Men and women carried hip flasks. Agents in Pittsburgh discovered people carrying one-gallon flasks curved to fit around the chest and stomach. The government never even came close to eradicating drinking. McGirr said Prohibition created "a new national obsession with crime, Prohibition—and the violence that came with it – pushed the federal government in the direction of policing and surveillance."

Prohibition agents raided homes, fraternal organizations and private clubs in their unrelenting hunt for illegal liquor. They even raided funeral processions. State police stopped a hearse carrying the body of an eighty-four-year-old woman and opened her casket searching for liquor. Troopers received a tip that bootleggers were smuggling alcohol from Pittsburgh to West Virginia in hearses.

Fraternal organizations in Pittsburgh, such as the Eagles and Moose, were targets along with private clubs, funeral homes, fashionable parties, swanky hotels and charitable organizations. In 1926, agents arrested forty people at Eagle lodges across Pittsburgh and then raided eighteen lodges of the Loyal Order of Moose. One of the lodges had a wildcat brewery installed in the basement protected by a twenty-five-inch-thick door.

Agents discovered liquor hidden in the chair of the Exalted Ruler of one Moose lodge. Agents even raided a meeting of the Amen Corner, a charitable organization founded in Pittsburgh in 1870 whose members included politicians, lawyers, judges, physicians and business leaders. The raid was carried out because agents discovered liquor at their meeting.

"Rottenness and corruption travel from the top down, not the bottom up," said Harold Wilson, assistant Prohibition administrator. "These bluebloods are violating the law just as much as the denizens of the underworld are who shoot craps in a back alley."

Floating speakeasies were another way bootleggers tried to provide alcohol. The palatial "Flotilla Club" was a floating casino with liquor, dice tables, slot machines and roulette wheels. In 1930, thirty agents wielding sledgehammers stormed the 120-foot-long vessel as it floated along the Allegheny River with four hundred people on board.

"Don't be alarmed," shouted a federal agent according to an account of the raid of the club in the *Pittsburgh Press*. "It's just a federal raid. Leave your liquor where it is and get out." Patrons began tossing their cocktails and bottles of beer overboard before agents seized five gallons of moonshine and barrels of beer.

Political corruption led all the way to city hall. Bootleggers paid politicians and the police to protect bootleggers, prostitution and gambling that was entrenched in Pittsburgh as well as in the towns along the Allegheny, Ohio and Monongahela Rivers.

Muckraking journalist Walter Liggett termed the city the "metropolis of corruption" because of the amount of graft and vice in municipal government. Despite constant federal raids, Pittsburgh remained "wringing wet."

"There is probably more vice to a square block in Pittsburgh, with a perfectly brazen political alliance between big business on one hand and blind piggers on the other which has no parallel in the United States today with the exception of Philadelphia," wrote Liggett in his book *Metropolis of Corruption*. Police served as a collection agency for politicians while Republican ward chairmen sold the rights to operate speakeasies, gambling parlors and houses of prostitution to the highest bidders. Police officers drank in speakeasies and held drunken parties in police stations.

Liggett blamed the city's political and industrial leaders for allowing the corruption to fester and singled out Andrew Mellon as the chief culprit. Mellon was the U.S. Treasury secretary and the man tasked with enforcing Prohibition.

Pennsylvania was a one-party state, and Pittsburgh was a one-party town controlled by Mellon and his nephew William Larimer Mellon, who founded Gulf Oil. The Mellon machine was not a machine in the strict political sense. The Mellon family fortune made people listen. The Mellons didn't make demands, but their wishes were granted. They financed campaigns, controlled large voting blocs, dispensed patronage and picked candidates they could support.

Bootleggers helped fund the election campaign of William Vare of Philadelphia for the U.S. Senate in 1926. After Senator Boise Penrose died in 1921, George Wharton Pepper was appointed to fill out the unexpired term.

Vare won the election but the Senate refused to seat him because of questions about the source of his campaign donations. Outgoing governor Gifford Pinchot charged that Vare should not be seated because his election was "partly bought and partly stolen." Vare had received nearly $800,000 in contributions, and Senator David Reed of Missouri called for an investigation into the financing of Vare's campaign.

Journalist William H. White of Pittsburgh testified before the committee that a $2 million slush fund, financed by the owners of speakeasies, saloons and brothels was spent to boost Pepper and Fisher "under the eyes of the police." Pittsburgh mayor Charles Kline, said White, threatened to fire any city employee who didn't support Pepper

"If you don't like Pittsburgh bread and butter, go to Philadelphia and Vare and get it," Kline said. "I'm asking every man on our payroll to come to our aid. Notwithstanding, we have a civil service law. I'll not keep a cheater for five minutes," according to a 1961 article in *Pennsylvania History* magazine about Vare's election to the senate.

The *Milwaukee Sentinel* found the story about corruption in Pittsburgh amusing enough to carry it.

"How do you account for such an organization in Pittsburgh maintaining its power?" White was asked. "I really don't know," he said. "Everything seemed to run wide open during the campaign."

"What happened when the Prohibition Director was transferred to Philadelphia?" Reed asked. "Well, they say the saloons had good beer."

6

Mob Rule

Martin Burke, a dapper Irishman, considered himself a businessman even though he was headed to prison for bootlegging. He owned a restaurant, saloon and hotel, but it was liquor that made him a millionaire. His reign in the early years of Prohibition ended in 1923, when he was shot as he answered the front door of his home. Burke was facing a thirteen-month federal prison sentence for violating liquor laws when he was murdered. He was meeting with four men and his twenty-five-year-old housekeeper when the doorbell rang. One bullet ripped into his heart, and he died a few minutes later. His companions heard the killer yell, "I got you now."

Burke was one of four men who conspired with an Ohio distiller involving two thousand cases of whiskey worth $250,000. The shipment was supposed to be used for bottling medicinal liquor, but Burke diverted the liquor for his bootlegging operation. Burke had boasted that he had evidence against others who were not charged in the plot and threatened to go public with the information. Three cohorts who went to prison believed they were cheated out of their share of the loot by Burke and were suspected in the killing although no one ever was charged with his death.

Burke became the "bootleg king" of Pittsburgh after Prohibition was enacted. Even though he lived in Pittsburgh, he also operated in Cleveland and Chicago. One of his lieutenants was killed in a shootout during a smuggling operation in Ohio. Burke's death left a void in the bootlegging industry, but that vacuum was quickly filled.

Pittsburgh can thank Italian dictator Benito Mussolini for bringing organized crime to America. In the 1920s, Mussolini drove the Mafia and the Naples-based Camorra out of Italy, forcing hundreds of Sicilian Mafiosi to flee to the United States between 1922 and 1929.

In America, the Black Hand, a group of Italian thugs, preyed on Italian immigrants in Pittsburgh. They extorted money from the wealthy by threatening their families with harm if their extortion demands were not met. They were experts with the stiletto, and their calling card was a letter with the imprint of a black hand. It was Prohibition that helped the Mafia prosper into a crime organization.

Nicola Gentile came to Pittsburgh in 1903 and joined the Black Hand and, at twenty-one, the Mafia. He killed a man in a crowded downtown saloon but escaped prosecution. He rose through the criminal ranks and overpowered the then-dominant Camorra, which controlled Pittsburgh rackets at the time. Gentile threatened the Camorra with an all-out, relentless war unless it bowed to his leadership. The Camorra capitulated, and the Mafia became entrenched in Pittsburgh neighborhoods such as Larimer, the Hill District and Homewood.

Gentile was ordered to face a mob tribunal in Chicago after a competitor, Giuseppe Siragusa, leveled secret accusations against Gentile. Gentile faced the ruling mobsters denying the charges and threatening to cut off the head of the person making those allegations. Al Capone admired the brash, young thug and intervened to save his life. Gentile went on to become a leading member of the mob in Kansas City and Chicago before returning to Italy, where he died in poverty.

Gentile was succeeded by Gregorio Conti, who ran a wholesale wine and liquor business in Pittsburgh in 1915. Conti was the leader of a group of Sicilians and Calabrians. A rival Neapolitan Camorra group in Pittsburgh was led by Ferdinand Mauro. On September 24, 1919, Conti was killed in his car allegedly because he had watered down liquor he sold to Mauro.

Salvatore Calderone became boss after Conti's death but relinquished control in Pittsburgh to Stefano Monastero, who took control over bootlegging in the 1920s until he was murdered. Luigi "Big Gorilla" Lamendola succeeded Monastero until he was killed. Partners Jack Palmere and Saverio "Toto" Amaroso were killed within eighteen hours of each other. Morris Curran, who tried to corner the markets on sugar and yeast, met his death in a hail of gunfire. Philip Fazio was acquitted of killing and beheading an associate of his bootlegging operation.

Giuseppe Siragusa was killed by Joe "the Ghost" Pangallo, who survived several assassination attempts and lived to die of natural causes. Other bootleggers fell like dominoes. Johnnie Daniels, Dominic Grillo, Dominic Caputo and John LaPaglia met violent ends. The Volpe brothers filled the vacuum for a short time until they were murdered. John Bazzano, another "yeast king," was killed shortly thereafter. He had consolidated the Sicilian and Calabrese clans in the city into one organization.

Stefano Monastero was considered the first crime boss of Pittsburgh until he was gunned down on August 6, 1927, according to the now-defunct Pennsylvania Crime Commission. Giuseppe Siragusa assumed the mantle until he was deposed as king by gunfire on September 13, 1931.

Monastero was born to be a mobster. His father, Pietro Monastero, a shoemaker, was one of eleven members of the Black Hand lynched by a mob in New Orleans after the death of police chief David Hennessy in 1890. Hennessey was ambushed in a section of New Orleans known as "Little Palermo" and died thirty-four hours later from gunshot wounds. Hennessy's dying words were "the dagoes did it," but he never specifically identified his killers. There were no witnesses to the killing and scant evidence, but police rounded up fourteen members of the Black Hand and charged them with Hennessy's murder. Pietro Monastero lived in a shack from where the attack was launched.

After a series of acquittals and mistrials the following year, an angry mob stormed the Old Parish Jail, chanting, "Kill them all." Pietro Monastero was one of several men dragged from jail; ropes were placed around their necks, and they were hanged from lampposts.

Monastero's mother took Stefano and his brothers, Sam and Lorito, and moved around the country before coming to Pittsburgh. The brothers worked as laborers and fell in with a group of young men forming the "Gas House Gang." Monastero soon became the gang's recognized leader, hijacking before starting bootlegging on Pittsburgh's North Side, a rough-and-tumble neighborhood filled with speakeasies, gambling dens and whorehouses.

Monastero and his brother Sam drove in their bulletproof car to St. John's Hospital in the Northside on August 6, 1929, to visit ailing gang member Charles Spallino, who was recovering from surgery. Spallino was a suspect in the killing of bootlegger Johnnie Daniels and was under indictment for trying to kill Joe "the Ghost" Pangallo by planting a bomb in Pangallo's car that blew him through the roof. Police suspected Spallino also may have been a target for assassination because his hospital room had been sprayed with bullets fired from the street.

The Monastero brothers were followed to the hospital by a convoy of bodyguards, but gunmen hiding in a nearby car ambushed the brothers, blasting them with shotguns as they walked to the front door. Stefano dropped to the ground. A gunman got out of the car, calmly walked up to the dying man and emptied his pistol into Monastero's head.

A heavily armed Sam Monastero fled through the hospital and was trying to leave out a back door when he was arrested by police. In his jail cell, a hysterical Monastero pleaded for a gun to shoot himself and then tried to hang himself with his belt. Stefano Monastero's funeral was lavish. Thousands paid their respects to the slain gang leader as a 125-car funeral procession carried his body to the cemetery followed by 10 vehicles filled with flowers. Several months later, Sam's body was found in his armored-plated car. He had been shot, and a towel tied in a death knot was wrapped around his neck.

Sam's death was the seventy-seventh unsolved murder in fifty-one months in Pittsburgh, and a Pittsburgh newspaper blamed corrupt politicians for allowing the slaughter to continue.

"Racketeering, protection of crime by politics, and not volunteer laxity of policemen, is responsible for the flouting of the law, the foundation of gang murder," read an editorial in the *Pittsburgh Press*. "Blame must be fixed on corrupt politics, and it is against this system that blows must be struck if the rule of gangland is to be broken."

Pangallo immediately became a suspect because he had sought permission from the chief of Pittsburgh homicide detectives to bring in hired killers from Detroit or Youngstown, Ohio, to kill Monastero. Pangallo was thrown out of police headquarters. Ray Sprigle, a reporter for the *Pittsburgh Post-Gazette* who won the Pulitzer Prize in 1938 for exposing that Supreme Court justice Hugo Black had been a member of the Ku Klux Klan, said he was responsible for the killing.

"I claim credit for the knocking off of the Monasteros," Sprigle said in a 1949 article in the *Pittsburgh Post-Gazette*. "I kept them on page one day after day. I played them up as the big tycoons of the underworld. Joe the ghost had to knock them off to keep his own self- respect."

Lorito Monastero disappeared from Pittsburgh after he was jailed for killing Stefano's mother-in-law, Angeline Casale. Shortly after his arrest, Lorito walked out of the city lockup but was recaptured a short time later. He was adjudged insane and confined to a mental hospital, but he escaped and was never seen again. Hospital officials kept his escape quiet for two months. Authorities suspected he had help in fleeing the institution and that he might have fled the United States.

Homicide detectives arrested four suspects in the Monastero killing, but the men said they couldn't speak English and refused to answer any questions about why their vehicle had bulletproof glass or contained a high-powered rifle and ammunition.

Another of Pittsburgh's most notorious bootleggers was "Pittsburgh Hymie" Martin, who was aligned with Moe Dalitz, a Cleveland gangster who later was known as the "Father of Las Vegas." Martin ran a liquor-smuggling network that shipped liquor from Pittsburgh to Cleveland, Detroit, Akron and Youngstown.

Martin was a dandy. With his slicked-backed hair and fancy suits, he liked to dine at fashionable restaurants in the company of beautiful women even though he was married. In 1931, Martin was arrested for killing disgraced former Cleveland city councilman William Potter. Potter had been acquitted the year before of stealing $33,000 in city money in a real estate scam while still in office. Potter was shot twice in the head with slugs fired from .32-caliber and .38-caliber pistols. His body was found in an apartment rented by Martin who witnesses testified they saw leaving the apartment building shortly after the murder. Martin denied killing Potter.

"I'm a bootlegger, not a killer," Martin said. "I haven't carried a gun for seven years. I'm a gentleman, a rum runner," he told the *Pittsburgh Press* following his arrest.

Martin was convicted and sentenced to life in prison. He served ten months before an appeals court threw out his conviction and granted him a new trial, citing an "amazing dearth of evidence." By then, one witness had recanted her testimony. Another admitted that police had paid her more a than dozen times for her testimony. Another claimed she was offered $5,000 by an anonymous party if she would change her statement. The jury, not sure whom to believe, acquitted Martin on June 16, 1932. He returned to Pittsburgh and opened a nightclub, but he disappeared from the city until 1960, when he resurfaced, overseeing gambling operations for Moe Dalitz along Florida's Gold Coast.

Luigi "the Big Gorilla" Lamendola arrived in Pittsburgh in the 1920s as a castoff from the Capone gang in Chicago. His nickname was derived from the fact that Lamendola was only five feet, eight inches tall but weighed 224 pounds. He was a gaudy dresser who liked to wear diamond-encrusted jewelry and had a reputation as a lothario.

Lamendola had a simple message for the owners of speakeasies: buy liquor from him or die. He muscled in on the territory staked out by other bootleggers using violence to get his point across. A rival bootlegger offered Lamendola a dozen cases of pre-Prohibition whiskey at $1,000 a barrel. Lamendola agreed to the deal, but when he tasted the liquor, he quickly spat it out. "That rat. This stuff is cut." Lamendola advised the man to think about returning to Italy, according to the *Pittsburgh Press*.

Lamendola had just closed his Hill District nightclub on May 19, 1927, when two men knocked on the door and beckoned him to come outside. The sound of children playing, along with the sounds of a passing trolley car, filled the street. Shotgun blasts tore into Lamendola from a passing car containing four men. A policeman responded and fired at the fleeing car. The gunmen returned fire, nearly striking a violinist playing in a nearby restaurant.

Police arrived and found $1,200 in one of Lamendola's pockets and four $1,000 bills in his wallet. Detectives picked up the diamonds that had spilled from his pockets into the blood on the street. His body was placed in a $10,000 coffin and shipped to Genoa, Italy, where Lamendola was buried.

Morris Curran operated a hardware store that was popular with bootleggers because the Russian immigrant sold plumbing supplies, copper coils, kegs, corks, funnels and bottling and cap machines they needed to make beer and whiskey. He also made a fortune from selling yeast, earning the title of "yeast king."

Curran worked both sides of the street. After selling essential whiskey-making equipment, Curran then told Prohibition agents who his customers were. After agents raided the stills, Curran would show up, give his regards for their loss of property and offer to sell them more supplies so they could resume their operations.

Pittsburgh newspapers speculated that Curran was "put on the spot" in a battle for control of sugar and yeast that reached a violent peak in 1932, when stores that sold the commodity or equipment used for distilling were shot up or bombed. One night, a car carrying four men peppered four stores in the Hill District and East End with shotgun pellets. The owner of one store, Pasquale Melagrano, sold equipment needed for distilling alcohol. "I sell bootleg supplies, yes, but I do not sell booze," Melagrano protested.

Curran set the price for yeast, a critical ingredient in making beer because of yeast's ability to convert sugar into alcohol. Curran drove some of his competitors out of business by underpricing them. Then, when his competitors fell by the wayside, he raised the price.

Curran had formed an association with other yeast dealers in Pittsburgh known as the "Keystone Company," but the organization soon dissolved after its members disagreed over pricing. That falling out led police to suspect that one of the members may have been behind Curran's assassination.

Attempts had been made on Curran's life before. The first came three years before his death in 1931, when he escaped blasts from a shotgun. In 1929, a bomb caused $100,000 in damages to the building housing his hardware store. Curran said he knew who did it but would settle the matter himself.

"If I was to die the next minute, I would truthfully say who blew up my place," he told the *Pittsburgh Press* in "Death of the Yeast King." "I would go right out there in the street and colar [*sic*] him and turn him over to the cops. Just say it was a case of business jealously and that the Black Hand had nothing to do with it. I'm going to stay right in the business until I make enough to quit. They can't make me quit."

Curran took an early retirement when he was shot while standing in front of his North Side home. As he lay dying, one of the four killers tossed the gun onto Curran's body. Police arrested Frank Abbott, who drove the getaway car, and Dominick Dugo after finding the car two miles from the shooting scene. Dugo was arrested as he was preparing to leave for Italy.

Two young girls saw two of the men leaving the scene and identified them as Pedrino and Angelo LaMantia. Police said both men were gunmen working for Chicago gangster Bugs Moran. Angelo LaMantia was a vicious killer who spoke English with a Sicilian accent. He was only five feet, eight inches tall with black hair, a dark complexion and brown eyes. Before arriving in the United States, he killed a jeweler in Sicily in 1922. He worked in Chicago for Joe Aiello, who hired LaMantia to kill Al Capone, but Chicago police learned about the plot and arrested LaMantia, who was carrying handguns, shotguns, dynamite and blasting caps.

After coming to Pittsburgh, LaMantia and Phillip Spaldino were suspected of killing bootleggers Saveria "Toto" Amoroso in 1931 and Antonio Lamendola in 1928. He was tried for the Lamendola killing but was acquitted. Chicago police wanted LaMantia extradited to Chicago to face trial for killing his brother-in-law, but the charges were dropped. At the same time, Italian authorities asked the United States to extradite him for the 1922 murder of the jeweler. In 1940, the Italian government withdrew the request. By the time the police charged LaMantia for the Curran murder, nine years had elapsed, and the two earlier witnesses could not positively identify LaMantia as one of the killers.

The streets of Pittsburgh were filled with blood in the 1920s and early 1930s, as police seemed powerless—or unwilling—to stop the killings since officers were often in the employ of bootleggers, providing protection for a price. Between 1926 and 1933, there were over two hundred gang murders.

Speakeasies were known as "blind pigs" or "blind tigers."

"There is a speakeasy at almost every door and gambling is widespread," complained a city councilman. "Either the police do not know their duty or they are not trying to perform it."

The Allegheny County jail was filled with bootleggers. The warden put them to work as cooks in the jail's kitchen using utensils seized in raids. "We want the boys to feel at home," said Warden John McNeil.

Roxie Long, whose real name was Rocco DiPippo, was a bootlegger who had been an inmate forty-two times in his long criminal career. He remained a bootlegger long after Prohibition ended, making moonshine into the 1960s. He was dubbed by the *Pittsburgh Press* and *Post-Gazette* as the "most arrested man in Pittsburgh" for a string of arrests and prison sentences dating to 1919 in nearly every story written about him during his long criminal career, which stretched into the 1970s.

Long was indicted in 1931 as part of a huge bootlegging ring that resulted in the arrests of forty-five people. Long became a government witness and testified against twenty-two defendants, earning the enmity of defense attorneys, who called him the "Al Capone of Allegheny County" and the "supreme weasel of the underworld." After he received a pardon on New Year's Eve in 1931, Long returned to bootlegging eleven days later and was arrested again.

Few of the bootleggers during this raucous period survived the gang wars, but several went on to become leading members of the Mafia in Pittsburgh. Louis Volpe was the last of the Volpe brothers to die. He was associated with the John LaRocca crime family. Frank Amato was arrested in 1929 for killing James Bruno with a shotgun in nearby Braddock. The charge was dropped when a local cop gave Amato an airtight alibi. Amato became a Mafia underboss in western Pennsylvania. He died in 1973.

Sam and "Kelly" Mannarino, brothers from New Kensington, just north of Pittsburgh, started out as bootleggers and sugar dealers and went on to become major figures in Pittsburgh's underworld. They once owned the gambling concession at the famed Sans Souci casino in pre-Castro Havana and supported Castro's revolution by attempting to supply guns from a National Guard Armory to the rebels in the mistaken belief Castro would return their casino, which had been seized by Cuban dictator Fulgencio Batista, to them.

Pittsburgh neighborhoods became bootlegger battlefields. The Hill District and Northside were particularly violent sections. Several Northside bootleggers and yeast merchants were gunned down in broad daylight by brazen gunmen firing shotguns. In addition to the Northside and Hill, the

Southside, Strip District and East Liberty were violent places where rival gangs shot it out for control of turf.

Bombings of speakeasies and distilleries were daily events in a fight for control of an underground industry that generated an estimated $50 million a year in profits. In 1920, police shot it out with bootleggers in the downtown area. "Bullets flew thick and fast and bounced off the pavement like water off a duck's back," reported one newspaper.

Police in 1928 feared a gang war, like the one then underway in Chicago and Philadelphia, would spread to Pittsburgh after the murders of two men, Tony Curcio and Mark Bartolotto. The bodies of Curcio and Bartolotto were found at Curcio's farm outside the city. Police found several shotgun shells near their bodies. Curcio had survived an earlier assassination attempt and accepted that he would die violently.

"I suppose someday they'll get me," he told reporters after the first attempt on his life.

The first indication that war was about to break out was an attempt on the life of Joe "the Ghost" Pangallo, who amassed a fortune extorting tribute from bootleggers. Pangallo was not a bootlegger and was known as the "underworld bogeyman" for his threats against bootleggers who failed to pay him a share of their profits. He also was an assassin for hire. Pangallo was arrested fifteen times for murder but had airtight alibis each time. Pangallo worked as a shoemaker. Even though he earned millions of dollars, he came to his shoe repair shop every day and worked for eight hours.

He was a fat, swarthy, foul-mouthed man whose clothes always looked like he had slept in them. His face had a constant five o'clock shadow, making him appear as if he never shaved. His appearance was in stark contrast to other well-heeled bootleggers, who loved finely tailored clothes and gaudy jewelry. Pangallo was a hard man to kill. He survived four assassination attempts from gunfire and bombs and died in bed of pneumonia.

7
Murder and Mayhem

Joseph LoBianco; his pregnant wife, Josephine; and his brother, Carmen were working in their Braddock store, ten miles east of Pittsburgh, one day in the fall of 1930. Josephine LoBianco was waiting on Louis Tomani, who had just walked into the store. Carmen was stocking shelves when the mom-and-pop grocery was riddled by a hail of machine gun fire.

A maroon-colored sedan sped up to the front of the small grocery and stopped. Gunmen sitting inside the vehicle opened fire, and Carmen LoBianco fell to the floor with ten bullet holes stitched across his stomach. The killers got out of the car and calmly walked into the store and raised their guns at Joseph. His wife tried to save her husband by lunging at one of the gunmen, who shot her twice before killing her husband. The only survivors were twelve-year-old Clarence Moore, who ran errands for the LoBiancos, and their seventeen-month-old son, who was asleep in another room.

"There were so many shots and people falling dead. I ducked out and ran home," said Moore in an interview with the *Pittsburgh Press* in what became known locally as the "Braddock massacre."

Carmen LoBianco was taken to a hospital, where a priest administered the last rites and asked him if he knew who the killers were. All Carmen could answer was "He wanted a pound of sausage, then boom, boom, boom" before his voice trailed off, according to the story.

Police chased three men and a woman in the car as they headed toward Pittsburgh. Witnesses later saw the four individuals jump out of the vehicle and into some nearby bushes. Investigators wondered why a small, mom-

and-pop grocery store would be the target of such a shooting spree. When police searched the store they found their answer.

The store's stock contained large quantities of yeast and sugar, and a search of Joseph LoBianco's home revealed a five-hundred-gallon still and ten thousand gallons of mash, along with a number of checks made out to James Volpe, the brother of the biggest bootlegger in the Turtle Creek Valley, John Volpe. Investigators suspected the store was a front for the Volpe bootlegging operation. Detectives found five checks totaling $1,800 from LoBianco to James Volpe over a five-week period. Volpe told suspicious detectives that he had loaned LoBianco money to open his store

"This is plainly a racket murder," Allegheny County coroner W.J. McGregor told the *Pittsburgh Press*.

Detectives ran out of clues, reaching a dead end in their probe. The case never was solved.

Even the man tasked with enforcing the Volstead Act, Treasury secretary Andrew Mellon of Pittsburgh, took a lax approach toward enforcement of Prohibition. Mellon owned a whiskey distillery, making him suspect in the eyes of the drys and temperance groups. Mellon was the third-richest person in the United States at the time, behind John D. Rockefeller and Henry Ford. His wealth was estimated at $400 million. He had interests in stalwart Pittsburgh financial institutions, such as Mellon Bank, U.S. Steel, Gulf Oil, Alcoa, Koppers, the Pittsburgh Coal Company, Pittsburgh Plate Glass and the Carborundum Company.

Bootlegger Philip Fazio said he paid $350,000 to politicians for protection. In a front-page article that he wrote for the *Pittsburgh Press*, Fazio detailed how he paid $10 in bribes from every $25 barrel of beer that he sold. Fazio said he kept moving his brewing operations around the city because politicians kept demanding more in payoffs.

"My advice to anyone who has an idea of going into the bootlegging business is to stay out," he said.

Later, a police lieutenant and two officers were indicted by a federal grand jury for assaulting two federal agents in city hall. Whiskey also was used as an inducement to buy votes. During one campaign, two thousand small bottles of moonshine— "liquid campaign cards"—were handed out to voters to buy votes.

Jack Palmere became the new king of yeast supplies following Curran's murder. In 1931, Palmere got out of his car to talk to someone when a gunman came up from behind him and fired one shot into the back of his head. His partner, Saverio "Toto" Amaroso, died eighteen hours later.

Palmere's base of operations was Pittsburgh's Hill District. The Hill had an international flavor in the 1920s and '30s. After the Civil War, the Irish immigrated there, followed by the Germans. In the 1880s, Italians and Slavs came as part of a mass migration from southern and eastern Europe to work in the mines and mills. Then Russian and Polish Jews arrived along with Syrians and Lebanese. A visitor could tell which neighborhood he was in by the aroma of ethnic food.

The Hill was infested with saloons and speakeasies all supplied by bootleggers who purchased their yeast from Palmere. There was so much bootleg liquor available in the Hill that it could be purchased at barbershops, newsstands, drugstores and dry cleaning shops, much to the chagrin of legitimate businessmen who believed the dives were bad for business. The Hill also was a dangerous place. Several bootleggers were gunned down in the Hill, and a black Prohibition agent was even shot while walking with his wife along a street in what police believed was retaliation for the agent's participation in raids on Hill speakeasies.

Businessmen and the clergy chafed at the lawlessness, but efforts to clean up the neighborhood were unsuccessful because the cops and politicians wanted it that way. The Reverend A.V. Hightower led twenty-five federal agents on nearly two dozen raids of Hill District stills. Police magistrate John Verona, a power in Hill District politics, threatened Hightower for interfering with the liquor business.

"This thing must stop," Hightower told the *Pittsburgh Courier*. "How can we rear our children decently amid such wicked environments?"

When Palmere heard that Curran was dead, he sat quietly in his speakeasy and sought out two of Curran's lieutenants, Toto Amaroso and Little Joe Spinelli. Palmere built a large distillery in a barn outside Pittsburgh. When New York City mobsters came to Pittsburgh and offered to buy Palmere's million-dollar-a-year yeast business, he refused.

Palmere learned through the underworld grapevine that there was a contract out on his life, so he began avoiding his old haunts. He never slept in the same place twice. His reign as "yeast king" was brief. He was walking along the street with a friend, Joe Colelli, on October 7, 1931, when a gunman calmly walked up to Palmere and shot him in the head. "The bullets whizzed past me. I thought I was killed," Colelli told police, according to accounts in city newspapers. When police searched Palmere's body, they found he was wearing a $2,000 diamond ring, and his pockets were stuffed with thousands of dollars.

His funeral also was lavish. Fellow bootleggers sent flowers and their condolences but stayed away from the funeral procession. Detectives staked out the service, but only a few women dressed in black prayed inside the darkened church during the Requiem Mass.

Eighteen hours after Palmere was killed, Amaroso was dead. The last man to see Amaroso alive was Spinelli, who stabbed and strangled Amaroso before wrapping his body in a blanket and setting it ablaze in a Lover's Lane just outside Pittsburgh. Spinelli's real name was Charles Spallino, and it was Spallino who was in the hospital recuperating from surgery when Stefano Monastero was ambushed and killed outside the hospital.

Spinelli had served as bodyguard for Palmere and Amaroso. On the night Amaroso was murdered, a man fitting Spinelli's description asked a farmer if he could stay at his house, which was located near the area where Amaroso's body was found. Detectives also were searching for Amaroso's cousin George Caffera, who had disappeared from his Turtle Creek restaurant; police suspected he also may have been murdered. Detectives found evidence that Caffera had left his restaurant in a hurry because they found his coat with $900 hidden in the lining and his car was packed for a long trip.

A grand jury indicted Spinelli, but he later surrendered, claiming to have been living in New York City at the time the two men were murdered. Spinelli never went to trial and later was released because the district attorney said every prosecution witness against him was missing.

When Joe Siragusa learned that Palmere was dead, he filled the void. Siragusa was a man with a keen mind for business and an unlikely candidate to be a racketeer. He arrived in the United States from Palermo and opened a successful bakery in Pittsburgh's Bloomfield neighborhood. Eight years later, he sold the business and opened a sandwich shop near the freight yards in the Strip District. The shop also was a success because of the railroad workers who ate lunch there every day.

In 1928, Siragusa sold the shop and opened the Empire Yeast Company, selling one ton of yeast each day to bootleggers, who made up the bulk of his clientele because yeast was needed to make beer. Siragusa became wealthy, building a $50,000 mansion with a clubroom in the basement that featured card tables, thick rugs, large, cushy chairs and a wine room filled with his favorite vintages.

Siragusa began underselling his competitors by selling his yeast at twelve cents a pound. His rivals complained and demanded a meeting to discuss setting a more equitable price schedule. Siragusa refused to compromise, and the other dealers left vowing revenge.

On October 7, 1931, Siragusa's wife went to Sunday Mass, leaving her husband at home in his basement clubroom. Siragusa was shaving when he heard a noise and turned to see three gunmen facing him. They fired a volley into a startled Siragusa who staggered against a wall as the slugs tore into him. He knocked down some religious pictures and stumbled toward a stairway, grabbing rosary beads that had been hanging on the post. Siragusa fell down on the floor, his face covered with shaving cream, as his pet parrot squawked, "Poor Joe, Poor Joe." Witnesses told police they saw a car in the neighborhood with New York license plates that was registered to a New York mobster. The gangster was brought to Pittsburgh; however, witnesses could not identify him, so he was released.

The public was infatuated with the gang warfare going on in Pittsburgh, and city newspapers reported on their homes, cars, political connections and speakeasies, as well as how they died. When Al Capone came to Pittsburgh in 1930, rumors began that the Chicago gangster was setting up operations in the city, but his visit was strictly social. After serving a year in prison for a weapons violation, he arrived in Pittsburgh in March to visit a friend, McKees Rocks racketeer Edward Cerceo, whom he had met in Florida. Capone stayed one night at a McKees Rocks hotel, handing out $100 bills to children. Newspapers reported Capone "was quite at ease and very friendly although not soliciting too much publicity."

Most bootleggers began their careers as young men. Philip Fazio became a bootlegger at nineteen. He first went to prison at seventeen, serving two years for robbery and weapons violations. He was in and out of jail between 1919 and 1950, serving time for state and federal bootlegging convictions.

Fazio was charged in 1930 with killing an associate, William "Stuttering Bill" Gregory, and cutting off his head. Gregory was supposed to deliver a shipment of liquor to Cleveland but instead sold the load to a rival gang of bootleggers. When Gregory returned to Pittsburgh, he told Fazio the truck had been hijacked. Fazio didn't buy the tale and began plotting Gregory's punishment. Gregory earned the nickname "Stuttering Bill" because he stuttered when he was drinking heavily.

Although Fazio had an alibi for the night of Gregory's murder, he was charged the next day after detectives found his fingerprint on a lightbulb and window cord at the crime scene, an old warehouse Fazio used to make whiskey and beer. Gregory's blood also was found on a light socket. Investigators discovered that Fazio had spread lime on the floor and walls of the warehouse where Gregory's blood had splattered.

Jack Molena, the star witness for the prosecution, was another associate of Fazio's who testified that Fazio tried to recruit him to help kill Gregory for $200. Molena testified that Fazio's plan was to hit Gregory in the head while Molena would strangle him with the cord. City newspapers tantalized readers with word-for-word details from court testimony about the gruesome killing.

"Let's kill Bill," Fazio asked.

"No, I'm afraid of him," Molena said.

"Oh, it will be easy," Fazio replied.

Molena also testified that Fazio tore the flesh off Gregory's body to remove identifying tattoos before stuffing his body into a barrel of cabbage. Despite the evidence and Molena's testimony, Fazio was acquitted.

8
The House of Volpe

John Volpe was the crown prince of bootleggers during the worst years of the Great Depression. He reigned over a liquor empire that stretched from the gritty steel towns and coal patches of the Turtle Creek Valley into the city of Pittsburgh. Volpe, who was born Giovanni "Prince John" Volpe in Agropoli, Italy, in 1894, claimed to have descended from Italian royalty.

"Not only are they princes in the American sense of the word, but the Volpes are princes in their own right," said a fawning politician introducing the brothers at a social gathering, as recounted by a later newspaper story.

There was nothing regal about John Volpe and his seven brothers. They were politically powerful men who used violence and bribes to bend people to their will. Judges, police officers, prosecutors, magistrates and attorneys were among their friends. In return, Volpe helped them remain in office by delivering votes and campaign contributions for their reelection.

Ignazio and Rose Volpe raised eight sons and a daughter in Wilmerding. John, James, Arthur, Amleto, Joseph, Guy, Louis, Caeser and daughter Clara made up the Volpe clan. Ignazio was born in Agropoli, a town along the Gulf of Salerno in southern Italy. The name "Volpe" in Italian means "fox" or someone who is a crafty person.

On a July day in 1932, an unarmed John Volpe left a Hill District coffee shop just as three men shot and killed him and two of his brothers, triggering a string of revenge killings that led detectives to Italy in search of the killers. The deaths of the Volpes were among 105 unsolved murders related to bootlegging in Pittsburgh over a five-year period when city government was ruled by an unholy alliance of gangsters, bootleggers, crooked cops and corrupt politicians.

"If the crime and corruption of Pittsburgh were not so well organized the city would probably rank ahead of Chicago in popular disrepute as the Bad Boy of American cities," wrote R.L. Duffus, a writer for *Harper's Magazine* in a celebrated 1930 article "Is Pittsburgh Civilized?" "In Pittsburgh the underworld can and often do murder one another, but gangster methods are for small fry."

The headquarters for the Volpe organization was the Rome Coffee Shop in Pittsburgh's Hill District, a hotbed of crime and political corruption during Prohibition. The Hill was known as Little Harlem because of the nightlife. Nightclubs with names like the White Cat, the Devil's Cave and the Harlem Casino flourished. Jazz music drew mixed-race crowds to black-and-tan clubs like Derby Dad's, the Little Paris and the Paramount Inn to listen to Ella Fitzgerald, Louis Armstrong, Dizzy Gillespie, Mary Louis Williams and Earl "Fatha" Hines. The most famous of all the clubs was the Crawford Grill, which became a mecca for visiting musicians and was owned by a former bootlegger-turned-sportsman, Gus Greenlee.

Drinking, said Harvard historian Lisa McGirr, had been confined to saloons, but Prohibition created nightlife in cities like Pittsburgh. Speakeasies and cabarets appeared throughout the city, but the Hill District was where the action was. Getting into a speakeasy was complicated.

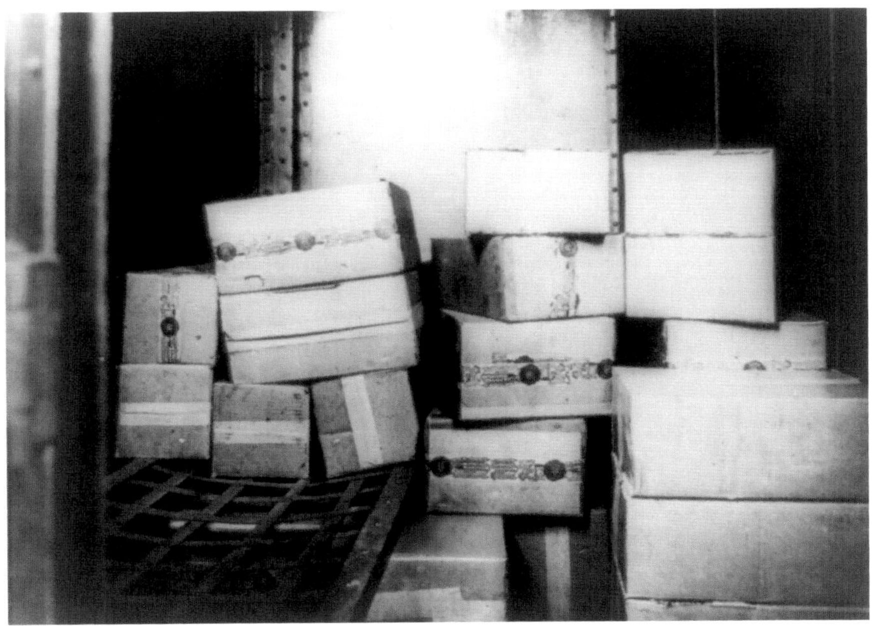

A cache of whiskey seized during a raid. *Library of Congress.*

"You had to knock on five doors and go through 10 houses to get in them," said John Brewer Jr., a Pittsburgh author, in his book *Pittsburgh Jazz*. "The password usually started with a 'd' and ended with an 'r.' That was dollar."

A Pittsburgh magazine, the *Bulletin Index*, captured the atmosphere of the clubs. "In an air of clatter, nickel-in-the slot phonograph, stale tobacco smoke, latticed arbors, lurid back bar murals and alcohol blur, the bar holds up a few loquacious clots of men on the two-by-four dance floor is dotted with a few wildly gyrating couples," reported the *Bulletin Index*. "Off in a corner, a girl with a guffawing party, suddenly breaks into 'Why Do You Do Me Like You Do' in a husky hi-de-ho voice. The inevitable hunched ring of young bucks intent upon pinball games never turned a hair."

The Turtle Creek Valley was a railroad town until George Westinghouse purchased five hundred acres stretching from Wilmerding to East Pittsburgh and built two factories that manufactured electric turbines and airbrakes. The valley lies east of Pittsburgh along a tributary of the Monongahela River where General Braddock was defeated at Turtle Creek in 1753, allowing the French to retain control of the Ohio Valley. The region is composed of a string of small towns that includes Wall, Rankin, East Pittsburgh, Swissvale, Pitcairn and Wilmerding.

Wilmerding was a violent town that was "beyond control" of local police and elected officials. Bootlegging, murder, gambling and blackmail flourished largely because of the power of the Volpe family. When federal agents raided a speakeasy in Wilmerding, they subdued an interfering Wilmerding policeman by slugging him in the head with a blackjack. When the agents tried to leave town, a mob of five hundred surrounded them until reinforcements arrived.

Wilmerding police officers and elected officials were regular patrons at speakeasies. One borough employee died after drinking hot moonshine directly from a Volpe still while a policeman was nabbed in a raid unloading a liquor truck owned by the Volpes. One Volpe cohort pointed a pistol at the head of a justice of the peace after the official demanded the man post bond after running over a nine-year-old girl. People took vengeance against personal enemies at gunpoint without fear of police interference.

Prince John was covered with Teflon. He was charged with murder in 1919 but found not guilty. Volpe and his brother Guy were suspected of killing Harry Davenport, a Wilmerding constable and chief of security at Westinghouse. Davenport raided a Volpe-run speakeasy in the valley, earning the family's enmity. Davenport also was a constable with the legal authority to conduct raids and make arrests.

As Davenport was walking home from work in 1926, a car pulled alongside him. A shotgun blast knocked him to the ground. Two men got out of the car and struggled briefly with Davenport before shooting him in the chest. Davenport's wife, Katherine, heard the shots and saw a car speed away.

Katherine Davenport told detectives she saw an old car speed by after her husband had dropped her off at the house before parking the car in a garage. "I stood there under the arc light and they could have shot me just as easily," she said during the coroner's inquest.

His wife said Davenport told her that "gang would never kill an American. He told me that just before he raided that club last month." After the killing, five Wilmerding officials received death threats warning of "more murders in Wilmerding" after they posted a $2,000 reward for the capture of Davenport's killer. "Watch out for your life," read one letter. A local tailor told investigators he heard four men standing outside his Wilmerding shop arguing over who would kill Davenport. "Well, I'll kill the ——," said one man. "No, I'll do it," said another, according to testimony at the inquest.

John and Guy Volpe, along with Joseph Mandella, were arrested for the killing but later released after a Wilmerding police officer said he was talking to the brothers at the time of the shooting. District attorney Samuel Gardner told the *Pittsburgh Press* following the inquest, "They had very good alibis and we were unable to incriminate them."

One witness told detectives that Mandella had tried to buy a shotgun from him several weeks before Davenport was killed. Gardner claimed to know nothing about any vice or corruption in Wilmerding and had no plans to conduct any investigation except for Davenport's murder. He said the borough was "one of the cleanest in Allegheny County." On the day of Davenport's funeral, Wilmerding councilmen fired the police chief and nine officers after the brothers and Mandella were released from jail. John Volpe told reporters after the inquest that he was friends with Davenport and had no reason to kill him.

> *I have absolutely no knowledge or information with reference to the killing of Harry Davenport. I was just as much shocked and stunned when I heard it as anybody else. I cannot understand why my brother and Joseph Mandella or myself should have been suspected of being connected with the tragedy in any way. Harry Davenport was a friend of mine and we were on the friendliest terms. I feel my arrest and confinement in jail was unjust but now that I am released I am glad and any rumor or suspicion that any of us had anything to do with the crime has been thoroughly investigated and our innocence established.*

In 1924, John Volpe pleaded guilty to running a nuisance house and paid a twenty-five-dollar fine. Two years later, he was charged with assault, but the charge was dropped. That same year, he was charged with riot and assault, but the jury was unable to reach a verdict, and Volpe was never retried. In 1929, he was found not guilty on another assault charge and had federal counterfeiting charges against him dismissed.

John and his brother, Louis, were convicted of assault for beating up a newspaper editor during an election. Seven years later, he was indicted again for assault, but the charge was dropped. He also was charged with inciting a riot and assault and battery, but the charges were dismissed after he appealed and received a new trial.

John Volpe got into an argument with a federal agent after a government raid on one of the Volpe stills. Later, he and two brothers went to the Wilmerding police station, kidnapped the agent and drove him to a country road, where they pistol-whipped him and left him lying unconscious.

In 1927, John, Louis and James Volpe broke into the Wilmerding police station, demanding the release of a prisoner. When the officer on duty refused, they beat him. Charges were filed. Andrew Park was an assistant district attorney then, and the case dragged on for three and a half years. When Park became DA, the charges were dropped. When Park ran for reelection in 1931, his challenger, Ralph Smith, charged that John Volpe managed Park's campaign. In 1932, John Volpe killed a pedestrian in a motor vehicle accident, but a coroner's jury exonerated him of any wrongdoing.

The Volpes bought votes for their favored candidates by filling cellars with coal during the winter, providing food for hungry families and buying presents for children at Christmas. People who couldn't pay their rent went to the Volpes. Out of work? The brothers could find someone a job because of their political connections. One brother was a councilman in Wilmerding. The brother-in-law was the chief of police.

In 1929, John Volpe founded the Workingman's Party and proposed a slate of candidates for election in Wilmerding. James Volpe won a seat on council along with another Volpe-backed candidate, as well as a tax collector and justice of the peace.

The Volpes invested in nightclubs, peddled bootleg liquor and controlled the lucrative numbers racket that first surfaced in the Hill District in 1926. The brothers, their wives and children lived together in an apartment building in Wilmerding.

The Volpes invested in legitimate businesses using public officials as partners. When the brothers opened the Fox Neon Sign Manufacturing Company in 1931, the chairman of the company's board of directors was a former superintendent of roads for Allegheny County. The firm's treasurer was the Allegheny County Clerk of Courts.

Their father, Ignazio, prospered from running a wholesale fruit business but turned the business over to his sons so he could return to Italy. Before their father left in 1929, his sons threw a lavish going-away party for him that was attended by local mayors, Allegheny County officials, district attorney Park, the superintendent of police for Pittsburgh, assistant district attorneys and a number of prominent attorneys.

In the fall of 1931, the Volpes displayed their political power by calling a meeting of every candidate running for office at Wilmerding's Philaretic Hall. The candidates included Allegheny County commissioners, four judges, the district attorney, the clerk of courts and the county controller. After the meeting, the clan threw a party. Every Volpe-backed candidate was reelected, but the results were voided because three hundred ballots were filed before the election was held. Investigators discovered that 125 of the voters didn't exist, and 4 were deceased.

Volpe began expanding his operation in early 1932 by encroaching onto territory controlled by competing bootleggers in Pittsburgh. In the spring, he called a meeting of his rivals at a Pittsburgh hotel to tell them he was taking over and would establish a price schedule for yeast, sugar and liquor. Members of a Northside gang refused to listen to Volpe's plan, telling the squat gangster to "go to hell."

John Bazzano had his own reasons for sticking with John Volpe. Bazzano ran a million-dollar-a-year yeast enterprise. Bazzano had been a protégé of Nicola Gentile, a founder of the Pittsburgh Mafia. Bazzano became a rich man by providing yeast so bootleggers could brew beer.

Whenever a bootlegger was murdered, Pittsburgh newspaper reporters wrote he was "put on the spot" or "taken for a ride" by rivals. The phraseology was an antiseptic way of saying the victim died in a hail of gunfire. John Volpe was "put on the spot" by three gunmen on a July day in 1932 in the Hill District where Volpe held court every day in a rundown coffee shop in a building owned by his business associate, John Bazzano. Every day, except Saturday, he stopped by Frank Manna's barbershop for a shave and a shoeshine before walking to the Rome Coffee Shop. On Saturdays, he got a shave and a manicure.

Volpe, dressed in a lightweight blue-gray summer suit, silk shirt and black bow tie, walked into the barbershop on July 29. Hanging from his vest pocket was a watch with a fob that spelled his initials, "J.V.," in twenty-five diamonds. He also wore a six-carat diamond ring and a diamond-encrusted stickpin in his shirt. It was the lunch hour, and the streets were filled with pedestrians as street cars rumbled back and forth along the cobblestone streets.

The temperature that day was in the mid-seventies. The thirty-eight-year-old Volpe was prosperous even though the Great Depression had brought Pittsburgh industries to a standstill, leaving thousands without jobs or homes.

Manna's Barber Shop was located across the street from the Allegheny County jail, where Louis Volpe was serving a jail sentence for bootlegging. Charles Modarelli, a down-and-out numbers writer, walked into the shop and tried to hit Volpe up for a loan, but Volpe rebuffed him. "I'm pretty well cleaned out myself," Volpe said. "I just fixed a mortgage up for $2,600 for a widow," according to "Pittsburgh: The Dark Years," a *Pittsburgh Post-Gazette* account of the slayings of the Volpe brothers.

When Volpe went to pay the bill, he didn't have anything smaller than a $10.00 bill in his wallet, so a friend, Joe Tito, who also was in the shop at the time, paid the barber the $2.25. Tito was a bootlegger who also ran a numbers operation in the Hill District. Tito was considered a suspect by police in the Volpe killings, as well as in the mysterious disappearance and murder of Bazzano, but he was never charged and later would go on to own with his brothers the Latrobe Brewing Company in Latrobe, which produced the iconic Rolling Rock Beer.

Volpe left the barbershop and walked down Fifth Avenue headed for the Hill District and a rendezvous with his brothers. He stopped at a drugstore for a milkshake. He spent twenty minutes talking to Joe Frank, a nightclub owner, before resuming his walk along Wylie Avenue past pawnshops, grocery stores and laundries until he reached his destination. Volpe walked into the coffee shop to meet his brothers James and Arthur.

The Rome Coffee Shop was located in a rundown section of the Hill. It was flanked by a printing shop on one side and an abandoned storefront on the other. Inside, the shop's floors were covered with wood, and a large coffee urn sat on the counter where Santo Bazzano, brother of the owner, stood. A glass case in the front of the store was filled with cigars. Several men were sitting playing cards when Volpe walked in, and his brother Arthur sat at a nearby table eating a bowl of cornflakes. After talking with his brothers for a few minutes, John Volpe left the coffee shop and walked out into the street at 12:45 p.m. just as a blue Ford sedan pulled up in front of the coffee shop. Three rough-looking men wearing suits and straw hats got out of the vehicle and pulled pistols from their coat pockets. The men were no strangers to John Volpe. Giuseppi "Big Mike" Spinelli led the trio. Spinelli, who had been a captain in the Italian army, came to the Turtle Creek Valley from Italy after the war. Volpe set him up in the bootleg business, and Spinelli later served as Volpe's bodyguard. Volpe looked at Spinelli and knew this was no friendly visit. When Volpe saw the pistols, he made a run toward his custom-made Cadillac that he had parked near the coffee shop. Volpe thought if he could reach the car, he would be safe because the vehicle had bulletproof glass windshields.

Spinelli aimed and shot at Volpe, who fell to the sidewalk with three gunshot wounds to the chest making a perfect triangle. He fell against a passing pedestrian, Antoinette Fera, who immediately fainted. Volpe's twisted body lay on the sidewalk, his expensive suit wrinkled and his shirt filling with blood from his wounds. Then the gunmen entered the shop and continued shooting. James and Arthur were both shot in the head. The *Pittsburgh Post-Gazette* described the scenes that followed the shootings.

The men playing cards scrambled to escape, knocking over tables and chairs as they ran out a back door. When police arrived, the walls were pockmarked with bullet holes from the fusillade. Santo Bazzano cowered behind the counter crying hysterically, "I don't wanna be shot, I don't wanna be shot," reported newspapers.

A crowd filled the street, gawking at John Volpe's corpse. One of the most powerful men in the underworld was lying in the gutter, and people began hollering, "The Volpes have been shot!" Mounted police officers arrived to push back the crowd. City newspapers quickly published special editions as newsboys hawked papers on the busy street. "A Political Boss Reaches Trail's End—In Gutter," read a headline in the *Pittsburgh Sun-Telegraph*.

Paul Pischke had just finished lunch at a nearby restaurant when he heard the gunfire and saw John Volpe fall to his knees. Pischke had lost a leg in an accident and walked with crutches. One of the bullets had struck one of his crutches. "I heard the shots," said a barber in his nearby shop. "They sounded like cap pistols. I didn't pay any attention."

The Reverend John McGuigan, a Catholic priest, was riding on a passing streetcar when he saw Volpe fall. He jumped off and administered the last rites to the dying gangster. Alderman John Verona, whose office was a block from the coffee shop, knew the Volpes well. "I was shocked when I heard the boys were killed," Verona said. "They were my friends and gentlemen."

Detectives took Santo Bazzano into custody, but he claimed he could not identify the killers. Detectives also questioned John Bazzano, as well as Joe Tito and Joe Frank. Police found the getaway car a few blocks away and learned the vehicle had been purchased in Cleveland, Ohio, by a buyer using a false name. Detectives found the guns used in the murders wrapped in a newspaper inside the car. John Freyvogel, a Wilmerding funeral home director, received an anonymous phone call advising him to come to the Hill District because "the three Volpe brothers have been shot."

An outraged Mayor Charles Kline took personal charge of the investigation, assigning fifty-two detectives to the case. He called the killings "one of the most outrageous and brutal crimes in the history of Pittsburgh." He ordered a crackdown on the city's underworld, although that was mostly for the public and the press's benefit. Governor Gifford Pinchot offered the services of the Pennsylvania State Police to help solve the crime.

Kline's outrage didn't stem from the brazenness of the murders but over the fact that the killings could upset his carefully orchestrated system of graft and payoffs that not only enriched him but also police officers and other politicians who protected the Volpe operations. An editorial in the *Pittsburgh Press* cited the massacre as evidence of a link between the racketeers and elected officials: "It is indeed as if racketeers had developed a government of its own, administering its law even to the death penalty and with the authorities of the legitimate government on such occasions all too ready to remain complacent on the sidelines."

Police were working on several theories. One was that Spinelli and Volpe had a falling out after Volpe slapped Spinelli in the face following an argument over a woman. Spinelli, like Volpe, also was a dapper dresser whose custom-tailored suits hid the bulge of a shoulder holster.

Spinelli had been a close family friend of the Volpe family. He was in charge of the funeral arrangements for the youngest Volpe brother, Chester, who was killed in an auto accident on New Year's Eve 1931. Spinelli arranged a funeral procession of 250 cars followed by another 25 carrying flowers.

Another story making the rounds was that John Volpe had tipped off Pittsburgh police about the presence of several New York mobsters who were staying at a Pittsburgh hotel. The men were arrested. John Volpe had ties to New York City and frequently made trips to Coney Island, where he owned the concession for bathing suits and towels.

Pittsburgh newspapers were outraged over the murders committed in broad daylight on a crowded city street. "Allegheny County cannot tolerate rival racket armies which turned it into a private battleground," read an editorial in the *Pittsburgh Press*. "City police and detectives have too clearly demonstrated little can be expected of them." The *Pittsburgh Post-Gazette* reported the brazen killings didn't foster much confidence in police to solve the crime. "Are the racketeers so important to the political scheme of things that no one dares smash their power? The results of the police investigation may be summarized by a large zero."

At a coroner's inquest in September, reported by the *Pittsburgh Press* in detail, detectives produced testimony from an eyewitness to the killings who identified Spinelli as one of the killers. Police would not produce the witness in court, but a detective read her statement into the record. The mystery woman picked out Spinelli's photo from a series of fifteen mug shots police showed her. In her testimony, she recounted:

> *I met Spinelli just in front of the coffee shop the day before the killings. The next day I was 15 feet away from the front of the shop. I saw Spinelli talking to John Volpe. Suddenly there were sounds of shots from inside the coffee shop. John turned and started to run inside. Spinelli grabbed him by the arm, wheeled him around and with his gun only a few inches from his back, fired six shots into Johnny. Only a minute or two afterward, while Johnny was dying on the sidewalk, two men came out of the shop. They joined Spinelli and all three ran up Wylie Avenue toward Chatham Street.*

The news of the killings reached Wilmerding. The wives of the slain men rushed to Mercy Hospital in Pittsburgh. A Catholic priest was the first person whom Angela Volpe saw when she entered the hospital.

"Father, am I too late?" He bowed his head. "They are at the morgue," the priest replied.

James's wife, Angela, had brought a small religious ornament with her. "I slipped a 'happy death cross' into my pocketbook praying I could put it in Jimmy's hand if he were dying."

The widows, faces shrouded beneath black veils, went to the funeral home to view the bodies. Their cries and sobs were so loud they could be heard outside on the street. The coffins were arranged in a U-shape in the flower-filled room.

More than seven thousand people massed outside the apartment building where the Volpes lived, and more than fifty thousand went through the Volpe home to personally pay their respects. People stood on rooftops and fire escapes to watch the funeral cortege pass. Children skipped school to watch the event. "They were good to us at Christmas time. All the Mr. Volpes," said one child.

"It is not only the youngsters who will miss them, though for them it's like having their Santa Claus taken away," said one mourner. "The grown folks will miss them, too, because no matter what anybody says, they helped a lot of people."

The funeral service was devoid of any religious ceremony. The Reverend M.A. McGary, pastor of the Catholic church in Wilmerding, said only Catholics in good standing could receive the sacraments and the Volpes were not regular churchgoers.

Louis Volpe, who was serving a six-month sentence for a bootlegging conviction in the Allegheny County jail, went to the library to read an early edition of a Pittsburgh newspaper before asking to be returned to his cell. He was allowed to leave the jail for several hours to attend the funeral. He sat in the family home gasping and repeating to himself, "Oh, oh, oh."

Three hundred cars lined up for the funeral procession, followed by another seventeen vehicles filled with flowers sent from fellow gangsters from Pittsburgh and Chicago. The bodies of the three brothers were carried through the streets of Wilmerding, but the crowd was so large that police on motorcycles had to run interference so the hearse could get through town to the cemetery.

State troopers lined the roads leading to the Grand View Cemetery in McKeesport, where the youngest son, Chester, was buried. John's coffin was blanketed with roses. There were so many flowers at the funeral that the air was filled with their sickly sweet scent.

John's wife, Amelia, said, "They killed him because he was too good, too big hearted." Angela Volpe told a female reporter for the *Pittsburgh Press*, who was able to infiltrate the crowd to attend the viewing, that she had a premonition of her husband's death:

> *I was so frightened I woke up screaming. The screams awakened Jimmy and I told him of my dream. He said "Listen, Angie, don't be nervous about me. If anything is going to happen, it's going to happen anyway."*
>
> *Because he earned money and was generous with it, everyone was too ready to call him a racketeer, a Dapper Dan, and such names. But those who knew him, as I did, knew he had a heart of gold. He never turned down a person who wanted help. He gave money, food and clothing to half the people in Wilmerding who were hit hard by this depression. I didn't question him about his business but I hope that now that he is dead, people who talked about him and hinted this and that will leave him alone.*

Rivals began to chip away at the Volpe organization. In September, one of John Volpe's lieutenants, Attilio Pecora, was walking with his wife on a Saturday night in Wilmerding when gunmen riding in a car drove by and shot Pecora. Pecora ran the numbers racket for the brothers and was good for delivering 350 votes in Wilmerding on Election Day. Someone Pecora knew called out to him as he was walking and fired two shotgun blasts at him. He was shot 300 feet from the brothers' home. He staggered toward the Volpe house. Guy Volpe found a dying Pecora cradled in his wife's arms as Wilmerding police officer James Piper arrived.

"For God's sake, do something," Volpe pleaded. "Piper, do something."

When Dominic Caputo met a bootlegger's death in 1933, he left behind a letter identifying the killers of a dozen men over a five-year period, including the Volpe brothers. The letter was sent anonymously to police. It contained details of the murders of Domenico Grillo, John LaPaglia, Louis "Big Gorilla" Lamendola, Stefano Monastero and the Volpe brothers.

Caputo named John Aliberti, along with Mike Spinelli, as two of the three gunmen in the Volpe slayings. Aliberti and Spinelli both were former bodyguards for John Volpe, and whenever Volpe held meetings at the Rome Coffee shop, Spinelli watched the street, a gun bulging from a shoulder holster beneath his coat. Aliberti was always at his side.

Aliberti, who had been indicted for bombing a Pittsburgh nightclub and the owner's car, later died from sixty stab wounds. Investigators initially thought he had been killed by a shotgun blast since his body was so badly punctured. He had served time in a West Virginia prison for being an accomplice in the killing of a Pittsburgh bootlegger "because he knew too much." Along with Louis Zambrano, the two lured the victim across the border to kill him and set his body ablaze.

Aliberti's girlfriend, Viola Morin, was held by detectives as a material witness to his killing, but she refused to talk. Investigators believed she knew more about her boyfriend's death—and of the Volpe brothers—than she was willing to divulge.

"Certainly, I know more about Aliberti than all of you," said a defiant Morin, whose real name was Jemma Demino. "But I'm not going to talk and you can't make me." Morin was dubbed by the *Pittsburgh Press* as the "kiss of death" girl. She grew up in the Hill District. Her father was killed by police, and her mother was seriously wounded in a gun battle. Morin's husband, Arthur Ambrose, a Northside gangster, went to federal prison a month after they were married. She quickly divorced him. Then she became the girlfriend of John LaPaglia, a wealthy bootlegger whose body and nearly severed head was found in his luxury apartment. Police found a hatchet protruding from his skull. After becoming Aliberti's girlfriend, she swore off men.

"I'm done with men from now on," she said. "I guess I'm bad luck to my men."

Police had suspected that Spinelli, Aliberti and Aliberti's driver, Ralph Girdano, were the three gunmen who killed the Volpe brothers. Girdano was questioned but was never charged in the Rome Coffee Shop slayings.

Investigators raced to Cleveland in their hunt for the killers in the hope that learning who purchased the getaway car would lead them to the gunmen. Investigators caught a break when Spinelli's car was found parked in a garage in Mount Lebanon near John Bazzano's home. Two grocery delivery boys identified Spinelli as the man visiting Bazzano's house shortly after the murders.

When police searched the car, they found it was registered to a "Guiseppi Spinelie" of Wilmerding and had a police radio installed on the dashboard, allowing Spinelli to monitor police broadcasts during the citywide manhunt for him.

Police began an intensive manhunt but had no idea where he was hiding, even though they had received reports that Spinelli was seen in the barbershop where John Volpe had his last shave and at a Hill District restaurant. Police scoured the country for Spinelli before learning that he had made his way to Canada, where he sailed for Italy in September 1932.

He returned to his hometown of Agropoli, Italy, where he was living with his wife and two children when Italian authorities arrested him in November 1932. Agropoli also was the hometown of Ignazio Volpe, who had retired to Italy. Ignazio alerted authorities in the United States that Spinelli was in Italy. The United States tried to extradite Spinelli, who fought being returned for eighteen months. The Italian courts ruled that Spinelli had renounced his Italian citizenship after he arrived in the United States, but at the last minute, the Italian minister of justice overruled the court and said Spinelli was still an Italian citizen and the law did not allow him to be extradited. Spinelli would have to be tried in Italy.

The trial was bizarre because of the way it was held. In Pittsburgh, seven men and two women were brought into a secret hearing to testify against Spinelli. Four of the witnesses, whose names were kept secret, testified about the events that day in 1932. Their depositions were transcribed and then sent to Italy and read aloud in court. Spinelli was convicted in 1936 and was sentenced to thirty years in prison. On August 2, 1936, the Italian Supreme Court denied Spinelli's appeal. The United States revoked his citizenship. Spinelli reportedly died in 1959.

Without John, the surviving Volpe brothers no longer wielded power in the Turtle Creek Valley and continued to be hit by tragedy and misfortune. Guy Volpe, who ran the legitimate family produce business, was arrested for shooting a man in 1930. He became an alcoholic and died of a stroke in 1934. Whenever his name was mentioned, someone would comment, "Guy? He's just a banana seller," according to a *Pittsburgh Press* story about the tragic deaths in the family. Guy Volpe became the fifth of the eight brothers to die. Younger brother Joseph was arrested several times on bootlegging charges and assault. In 1933, Louis, Joseph and Guy were arrested for threatening a man who refused to allow them to use his store as a liquor warehouse. They were housed in the Wilmerding jail when they couldn't raise the cash to make their bail. Mallie Volpe was on the run from the law and went to Italy to visit his father, who died during the visit in 1936.

The Rome Coffee Shop was padlocked for nonpayment of rent. Over the years, it had housed a pawnshop and a junk store. The last tenant was a fortuneteller. In 1956, the wrecking ball removed the last traces of the gangland haunts of Luigi Lamendola, Jack Palmere and the Volpe brothers. A $14 million redevelopment project devastated the lower section of the Hill District to pave the way for Pittsburgh's Civic Arena.

9

Death in Red Hook

John Bazzano was the new boss in Pittsburgh, but a few days following the murders of the Volpes, Bazzano disappeared after taking a train to New York City, where he had been summoned at the behest of a newly formed commission of Mafia bosses to settle disputes between families.

Bazzano came to the United States from Italy in 1909 and worked in West Virginia and Johnstown, Pennsylvania, before settling in Pittsburgh. He joined the U.S. Army and served in World War I. He didn't have a criminal record, although he once was arrested for stealing sixty barrels of whiskey; the charges were dropped. After the war, he opened an olive oil import business, owned three movie theaters and built a business selling yeast to bootleggers that generated $1 million in revenue, making him wealthy and allowing him to live in a mansion surrounded by well-tended gardens.

Louis and Joseph Volpe complained to the commission that Bazzano was behind the murders because he feared John Volpe was trying to replace Bazzano as the boss in Pittsburgh. Lucky Luciano's underboss, Vito Genovese, summoned Bazzano to New York under the pretext that Bazzano was being honored at a testimonial dinner. He was accompanied on the trip to New York by Big Mike Spinelli and Joe Tito. They checked into a hotel in separate rooms. Bazzano's room was next to the one where Spinelli and Tito were staying. When Bazzano left the hotel the next day to report to the meeting spot in the Red Hook neighborhood of Brooklyn, Spinelli and Tito had already checked out of the hotel.

When Bazzano arrived at the meeting place, he quickly realized the grim-faced bosses were not happy with him. They confronted him about his reasons for the killings. "You have provoked great evil and have implicated others in this deed making them appear to be accomplices," Bazzano was told, according to a detailed article about the Bazzano murder in the *Informer: The History of American Crime and Law Enforcement*.

A protégé of Nicola Gentile, an early Pittsburgh Mafia boss, Bazzano kept such a low profile that Pittsburgh police had never heard of him. He owned the small coffee shop in the Hill District but lived in a mansion in the upscale Mount Lebanon neighborhood just outside Pittsburgh's city limits. Gentile, who once faced death before a mob tribunal in Chicago, escaped with the help of Al Capone. Bazzano took a page out of Gentile's book and began arguing defiantly with the Mafia bosses, thinking he could talk his way out of punishment. He defended his action, saying it was the right move to kill the brothers and demanded the mobsters declare outright war against the Neopolitans.

"We finally can eliminate these Neopolitans," argued Bazzano, according to the *Informer*.

The Sicilians controlled bootlegging and other rackets on Pittsburgh's North and South Sides while the Neopolitans controlled the East End. The Sicilians and Neopolitans fought for control of Italian neighborhoods in Pittsburgh as well as surrounding areas. The Volpes controlled the Neopolitan faction but angered Bazzano when they began expanding into the North Side and East Liberty.

According to one account, Santo Volpe, a mob boss from Scranton, Pennsylvania, and no relation to the brothers, and Albert Anastasia killed Bazzano and then dumped his body in the Red Hook section of Brooklyn at a site known as "Tin Can Mountain," a dumping ground for refuse, stolen cars and bodies. The area was named by Dutch settlers, who called it *Roode Hoek* after the red clay and the way the land formed a hook protruding from the Brooklyn shoreline. Al Capone had begun his criminal career in Red Hook as a petty criminal.

The *Pittsburgh Post-Gazette* described Bazzano's death in a 1932 article:

> *Bazzano's body, trussed up like that of a slain animal, with the head and arms drawn down between his legs, with 22 tiny stab wounds in his chest and the other end of the rope with which he was tied drawn tight about his neck, was found before dawn Monday morning in the middle of Center street, Brooklyn, in the heart of the notorious Red Hook underworld*

> *district. The maimed body, the hands and feet also securely bound, had been thrust into a burlap sack, and from the position in the street where it had been found. New York police believed that Bazzano had been murdered elsewhere and thrown from a speeding automobile in Center Street. The face of the murdered man, swollen by strangulation, still was distorted by the anguish of his torturous death....The New York police representative, who was first at the scene when Bazzano's body was found, denied the story told here that Bazzano's tongue had been severed, and a strip of adhesive plaster stuck across his lips.*

Santo Volpe was known as the "king of the night" and would become a Mafia chieftain in the anthracite coal fields of the Scranton and Pittston areas of northeast Pennsylvania. Anastasia was a ruthless killer who was known as the "lord high executioner" and head of "Murder Inc.," a criminal group suspected of carrying out between four hundred and one thousand contract killings in the 1930s and 1940s.

Pittsburgh newspapers caught wind of the investigation by New York City detectives, who found hotel bills with Spinelli's and Tito's names and immediately jumped to the conclusion they had killed Bazzano. "Bazzano Gangster Killers Known," blared the August 15, 1932 headline in the *Pittsburgh Press.* New York City police raided a party celebrating Bazzano's murder and arrested fourteen men, including four from Pittsburgh. A contingent of forty detectives nabbed the suspects, who included Anastasia and Paul Palmere, the brother of slain mobster Jack Palmere from Pittsburgh.

Four of the suspects—Carlo Spallino, Michael Bua, Michael Russo and Frank Adrana, all from Pittsburgh—were among those arrested in the Bazzano murder. Police said New York underworld bosses hired the four men to kill Bazzano. They "wined and dined" them and paid them $5,000 each. In August 1932, Pittsburgh police charged Spinelli with murder. Another suspect, John Aliberti, who was believed to be involved with Spinelli in the slayings, was murdered in what police believed to be retaliation for the Volpe slayings. Police in New York said they had enough evidence on the suspects to convict them of murdering Bazzano.

"We have circumstantial evidence against all of these men and some documentary evidence," said a New York police captain in an article carried in the *Pittsburgh Press.*

Detectives scoured Italian neighborhoods in Red Hook and found the ice pick used to stab Bazzano and the warehouse where he was murdered. The suspects were held without bond, much to the anger of defense attorney

Samuel Leibowitz, who once represented Al Capone and killer Vincent "Mad Dog" Coll. Leibowitz had a record of seventy-seven acquittals out of seventy-eight murder cases.

"This is the most wholesale homicide arraignment in the history of criminal procedure," Leibowitz said in the *Pittsburgh Press*, "and will be the most wholesale discharge of defendants for there is absolutely nothing against these men—absolutely nothing."

Leibowitz was right. The suspects were released because of lack of evidence. In Pittsburgh, agents from the U.S. Department of Labor began checking the naturalization papers of bootleggers and racketeers to learn whether they should be deported for possible fraud in the naturalization process. Murray Garson, a Labor Department official who deported a number of gangsters from Chicago, was assigned to Pittsburgh to determine whether of the city's racketeers were in the United States illegally.

The funeral for Bazzano wasn't as lavish as the services for the Volpes. Seven cars filled with flowers trailed another seventy-five vehicles filled with mourners. Bazzano's body was returned to Pittsburgh. His wife, Rose, thought her husband had gone to New York on a business trip. She sat in her home accepting condolences and muttering to herself, "John, come home."

10

"What This Country Needs Is a Good 5-Cent Glass of Beer"

President Hoover, vexed by the lack of enforcement of the Volstead Act, formed the National Commission of Law Observance and Law Enforcement in 1929 to study ways to bolster prosecution. The commission became known as the Wickersham Commission, named after its leader, George W. Wickersham, who was born in Pittsburgh in 1858 and served as U.S. attorney general under President Taft in 1909.

The commission produced a series of reports on crime, but the one that drew the most attention concerned bootlegging. Prohibition had corrupted police and politicians, the report noted. Local authorities refused to cooperate with federal agents. Organized crime and gang killings became national menaces. Government investigators couldn't stop the flow of liquor no matter how hard they tried, how many raids they conducted or the number of arrests they made.

Between December 1921 and September 1924, federal agents in Pittsburgh seized 7,000 gallons of alcohol, 5,000 quarts of whiskey, 300 gallons of moonshine, 1,200 gallons of wine, 105 quarts of bitters, 600 gallons of Jamaican ginger and 75 quarts of gin. They also destroyed sixty-five stills and seized 37,000 gallons of mash and 5,900 pounds of corn sugar. In a four-month period, agents seized 130,000 pints of liquor and more than 5,800 gallons of whiskey.

During the same four-month period, bootleggers produced over 100,000 gallons of moonshine each week along with 1,500 gallons of whiskey. In addition, between 5,000 and 6,000 gallons of Canadian whiskey were being smuggled into the city from Canada.

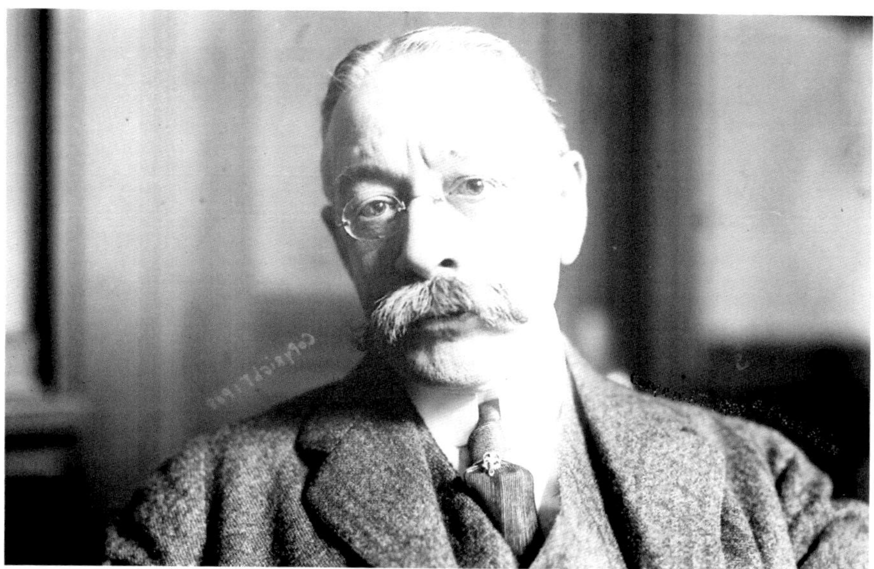

A portrait of George Wickersham, who chaired the National Committee on Law Observance and Enforcement, informally known as the Wickersham Commission, during the Great Depression. The commission's report cited police misconduct and corruption and urged more spending and effort to enforce the Volstead Act. *Library of Congress.*

Wickersham said the federal government gave inadequate support to enforcement. The courts were clogged with cases and cited a need for more judges and prosecutors to handle caseloads. The report was controversial because it gave impetus to repeal by reporting that the law should be revised. Two-thirds of all federal court prosecutions nationwide were for liquor law violations. There were more than fifty-four thousand prosecutions in 1921. By 1932, the figure had increased to more than ninety-two thousand. Adding to that number, 40 percent of those cases were appealed, further tying up judges.

In Pittsburgh, three-quarters of all cases in federal court were for Volstead Act violations. The prosecutions were a drain on the judicial system's budget. To reduce costs, judicial officials in Pittsburgh reduced the amount jurors were paid for serving. Witness fees also were cut, and the criminal court term was reduced from six weeks to four. Officials said it cost almost as much to house a federal prisoner as it did to feed a homeless person. The government spent $0.75 a day to keep one bootlegger in jail versus $0.90 a day to feed a person living on the street. James Doran, the national Prohibition administrator, said it cost taxpayers more than $460,000 a year to enforce the Volstead Act in western Pennsylvania.

"There is no case that gets colder than a Prohibition case," said President Hoover in news accounts following release of the Wickersham Report. "The witnesses leave and it seems harder to keep life in a liquor case than almost any other type."

The Wickersham Commission did not recommend repeal but instead urged spending more money and effort toward enforcement. The commission's recommendations were ignored. One recommendation caught the eye of Governor Gifford Pinchot and became the cornerstone of Pennsylvania's new liquor laws—the creation of a state store system. That recommendation didn't sit well with the drys, who believed the government was trying an end-run around the Volstead Act and pave the way to repeal the Eighteenth Amendment. The *Pittsburgh Post-Gazette* lamented the failure of the Wickersham Commission to recommend repeal.

"And so the present Volstead law will go on and on and the bootlegger and racketeer and the crooked political machine and the 'bought and paid for' judges, and the minor officials will continue to prosper at the expense of the citizens of our county, unless Congress overrules the president's recommendations and takes a sensible stand for a law," read the *Pittsburgh Post-Gazette*.

Prohibition advocates charged that Hoover had influenced the report by planting the seeds of repeal, which became a political issue in the 1932 presidential election campaign. Hoover publicly stood squarely with the drys, who praised him for his stand but privately decided Prohibition was a failure. Hoover lunched with Senator William Borah of Idaho, who was the leader of the drys in the Senate.

In a candid discussion between the two, Hoover told Borah the law was unenforceable and that he favored repeal with the decision to be wet or dry left with the states. "I stated the liquor question should be returned to the states," Hoover wrote in his memoirs. Surprisingly, Borah agreed. Hoover complained that the lack of cooperation between the federal and state and municipal governments made it difficult to make the law effective.

One of Prohibition's most ardent opponents was Dr. Samuel Harden Church, president of Carnegie Tech, now Carnegie-Mellon University in Pittsburgh, who railed against the Volstead Act throughout the time Prohibition was in force. He attacked the Anti-Saloon League and the Methodist Church for meddling in government affairs. He called the Volstead Act a "draconian statute" in a movement financed by "zealots, fanatics and bigots" backed by "their paid orators and professional agitators," in a 1925 article in the *North American Review*.

"It is humiliating to the soul to know that in a great nation like ours no man can take a purchased mug of beer, drink a whiskey, or a glass of champagne without violating the fundamental law of the land," Church said. His testimony was aimed at the "egotistical bigots" who were trying to dictate the public morals of the country.

Efforts at repeal had been churning in Congress ever since Wayne Wheeler, the influential leader of the Anti-Saloon League, died in 1927. By 1932, Congress had shifted its political gears with the election of Franklin Delano Roosevelt and began a stampede toward repealing the Eighteenth Amendment. Two factors gave added impetus to the movement. First, female voters mobilized under the Women's Organization for National Prohibition Repeal. Women in Pittsburgh began wearing scarfs with the slogan "Repeal the 18th Amendment" printed on them. The same slogan also began appearing on cigarette cases and lighters, lipstick and matchboxes.

Second, the Great Depression played a role. As the ranks of congressional drys thinned, farmers, who once supported Prohibition, wanted the law rescinded because of the economic affect it had on agriculture and the demand for corn, rye, barley and hops. Wets in Congress argued that repeal would create new jobs and tax revenue that would help keep state governments afloat financially and fund relief for the jobless and hungry. The first step toward repeal came when Roosevelt signed the Cullen-Harrison Act, a revision to the Eighteenth Amendment legalizing beer with 3.2 percent alcohol content.

Drys fought to the bitter end, adopting the slogan "No surrender, no retreat, no compromise." The debate became a question of law and order versus moonshine and nullification. Congressman Morris Sheppard, the father of Prohibition, said liquor "is the most dangerous character in our national life," in the May 1911 edition of *The American Issue*. No one in Congress was listening any longer to Sheppard and his supporters.

The *Pittsburgh Press* reported district congressmen were split over repeal. Harry Estep opposed President Hoover's plan to expand the power and scope of the federal court system to handle Volstead Act violations.

"I don't think Prohibition can be made successful under any conditions unless you call a law which requires expenditures of millions and setting up a national police force to hourly and daily interfere with the private lives of citizens," the *Press* reported Estep saying.

U.S. assistant attorney Raymond D. Evans in Pittsburgh said public opinion made it hard to enforce the Volstead Act.

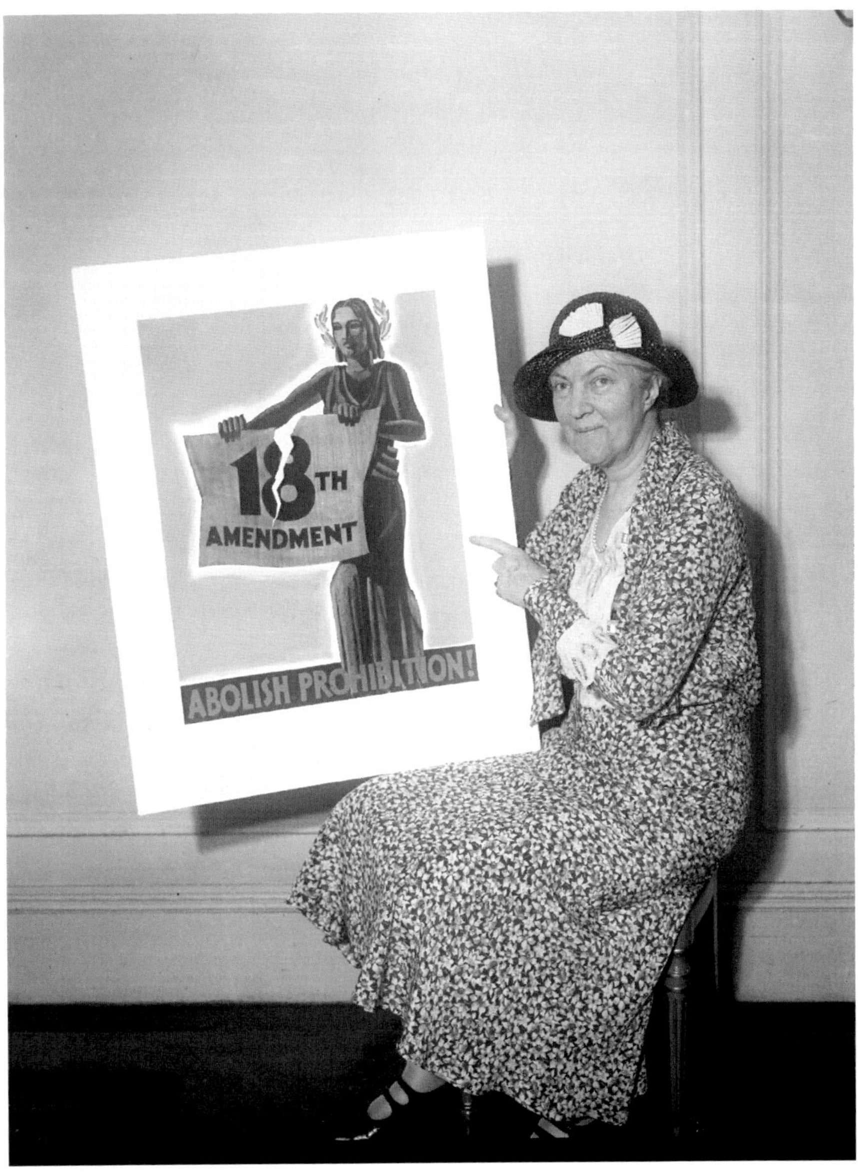

This page and opposite: After winning the right to vote, women became a major force in repealing the Eighteenth Amendment. *Library of Congress.*

"Public opinion in a given community either makes or breaks the enforcement of criminal law in that community," he said. The Great Depression gave the beer and liquor industries "the ammunition to give the drys a blow to the solar plexus."

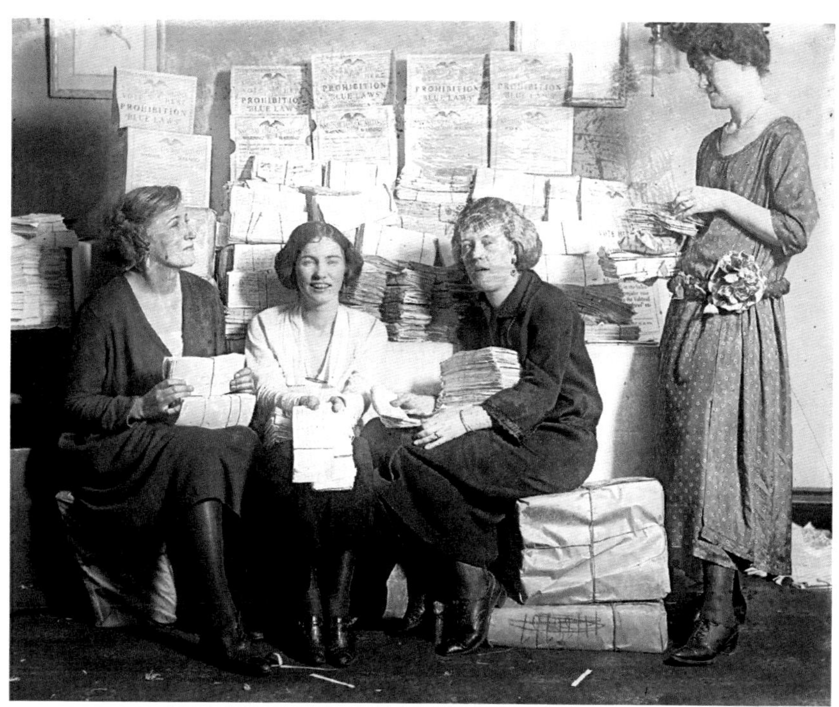
PROHIBITION
BLUE LAWS

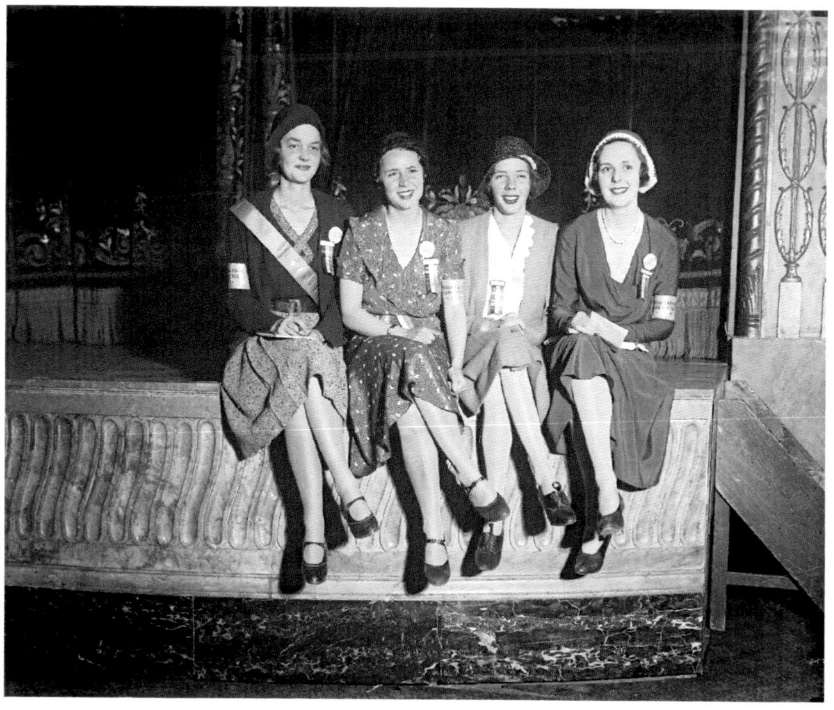

Candidate Franklin D. Roosevelt came to Pittsburgh in the fall of 1932, promising a huge throng at Forbes Field a balanced budget with hundreds of millions of dollars of new revenue generated by a tax on beer as soon as Prohibition was modified or repealed. Roosevelt, who liked a cocktail now and then, never believed Prohibition would work and thought it was a public policy miscalculation.

"We urge the enactment of such measures by the several states as will actually promote temperance, effectively prevent the return of the saloon and bring the liquor traffic into the open under the complete supervision and control by the state," FDR said.

"What this country needs is a good five cent glass of beer," said journalist H.L. Mencken, according to Garrett Peck in *Prohibition in Washington, D.C.: How Dry We Weren't*.

Within 288 days, Prohibition was repealed. The Democratic Party had made repeal part of its campaign platform in the 1932 election. State conventions were formed to ratify the Twenty-First Amendment rather than seeking approval through state legislatures. On December 5, 1933, the amendment was ratified.

With repeal looming, voting on whether to accept the Twenty-First Amendment began. Pennsylvania's fifteen delegates, led by Lieutenant Governor Edward Shannon, ratified the Twenty-First Amendment on December 5, 1933, ending Prohibition. Officials immediately sent two copies of the measure to Washington, D.C. One was sent by airplane and the other hand-delivered by a motorcycle policeman. Another was sent to Governor Pinchot, who was planning to make buying liquor difficult and expensive.

Repeal was met calmly in Pittsburgh, with police reporting few arrests. Philip Murray slept through the hubbub. He was the last person in Pittsburgh charged with bootlegging, for having a pint of moonshine in his possession. Murray fell asleep in his jail cell. When he awoke, Prohibition was over. A magistrate fined him fifty dollars and sent him on his way.

People lined up for blocks around Pittsburgh breweries, waiting to buy beer. Mill and factory whistles sounded as repeal officially ended. A crowd gathered at Sam's Restaurant on December 5, 1933, to await the end of the nation's long dry spell. The restaurant's owner installed a ticker-tape machine so patrons would know when Prohibition officially ended at 5:23 p.m. The *Pittsburgh Post-Gazette* dispatched reporters to bars and clubs to record the first person to buy a legal drink.

Otto Sogal wanted to be the first. He walked into Sam's to the cheers of the crowd and waited for the machine to ticker, reported the newspaper.

Sogal's goal was to be the first person in Pittsburgh to take a legal drink of liquor. But Sogal couldn't afford the fifty-cent price, so he opted to be the last person in Pittsburgh to drink moonshine for a dime.

> *I'm going to be the last man to drink a shot of "moon" at low prices. From now on I expect I won't be able to afford it. There'll be lot of guys drinking it tonight at fifty cents a drink but I'm going to be the last guy to swallow it down at ten cents and know what I'm getting. And just to make sure there ain't no time lost pouring anything, I ain't going to have nobody help me lift my elbow. I'm always in condition and I been giving myself intensive training for weeks. My arms work so smooth now I could take my teeth out with one movement. This is the greatest thing I have ever undertaken. I am not in the least perturbed. I expect to carry on with my accustomed services. If I can get another bottle after this one I will carry on even more.*

A *Post-Gazette* reporter described the scene as Sogal sat on the edge of his bar stool. The ticker began to clatter to life. "Get ready, Otto," someone yelled. "Here it comes." After three clicks from the machine, someone yelled, "Go," and Sogal, true to his word, guzzled the drink in a smooth motion. Cheers went up throughout the room. Then Sogal's eyes widened as he lunged forward, spitting the mouthful of booze onto the floor.

"You've ruint my record," he yelled. "I'll never get another chance. Ugh! That was bonded stuff you handed me."

The scene was much calmer at a Sixth Avenue restaurant reported the same *Post-Gazette* story. H.E. Wilson toasted the end of Prohibition by hoisting a martini, making him the first person in Pittsburgh to legally drink liquor, although a bartender at the Pittsburgh Athletic Club claimed he served the first drink at 5:31 p.m. "Here's to Prohibition. It was a helluva sight better than ain't having whiskey," said a patron.

Hotels and restaurants prepared for the onslaught of thirsty drinkers by offering the same prices for drinks as speakeasies. Some establishments continued serving bootleg liquor because of a shortage of bonded booze and passed it off as the real stuff. Cash registers clinked every two seconds in some places as crowds bellied up to the bar while bands played "Happy Days Are Here Again" and "Hail, Hail, the Gangs All Here." One speakeasy owner told the *Post-Gazette* he would miss "the good old days. Yes, we are going to have legal liquor and drinking won't be a sacred obligation anymore, it'll just be a bad habit."

Repeal didn't bring an end to violence or bootlegging. Police raided the Penn Shady Hotel and arrested Louis Volpe and thirteen cohorts for bootlegging after repeal was enacted. Two of the suspects arrested were accused of killing rival bootleggers. Ronald Cerotti was charged with the 1927 murder of Rosario Arcadia. Frank Amato was charged with the slaying of James Buono. Mike Bua, who had been charged then cleared in the murder of John Bazzano, also was picked up.

The home of Pittsburgh mayor John Herron was under police guard in 1933 after he ordered a police crackdown on bootleggers who continued to operate. The home of a Republican chairman in the Tenth Ward was bombed, causing $10,000 in damage. A plot was foiled to blow up the home of the chairman of the Eleventh Ward after five sticks of dynamite were found outside the house. The Ban Box nightclub, owned by Tom "the Greek" Contis, also was damaged by an explosion.

The vice crackdown imposed by Herron was lifted to refill the campaign coffers of Pittsburgh politicians, who faced a tough reelection challenge in the fall of 1933 by a slate of independent candidates. The lid was off, and speakeasies and gambling dens were allowed to reopen to generate a new stream of donations for elected officials.

The lack of police action triggered an outcry from the clergy. The Reverend Dr. Ray E. Snodgross of the Northside complained that detectives were unable to locate vice dens even though the public knew where they were in a scathing account in the *Post-Gazette* in May 1933.

"Detectives that are only half efficient and on the job but half of the time can find plenty of places on the Northside to be closed up," he said.

A price war over beer broke out in 1933. Louis Impellicceiri, forty-two, the owner of the Blue Arch Beer Garden, was shot to death. A roadhouse was bombed, and a beer distributor was threatened for cutting his prices. Another beer distributor had a brick thrown through the building of his business with a note, warning, "$1.30 a case or next a bomb."

The federal government, determined to end bootlegging after repeal, cracked down hard. Tax officials levied liens against bootleggers for failing to pay taxes. Joe Engelsberg, a political boss who served time for bootlegging, was hit with a $1.5 million lien.

There was some good news for bootleggers. The U.S. Supreme Court ruled that defendants charged with violating the Volstead Act before repeal was enacted could not be prosecuted. The ruling freed 250 defendants who had been awaiting trial in Pittsburgh and Allegheny County.

Pennsylvania immediately took advantage of repeal by imposing a two-dollar tax on each bottle of whiskey the state had seized from its owners since the start of Prohibition and held in storage. The liquor was reclaimed by its owners, but they had to pay the tax on each bottle. Guards were posted around distilleries to prevent liquor from being removed until the taxes were paid after one outraged distiller started shipping 200,000 gallons a day of liquor out of state to avoid paying the new tax. The state also ordered distillers to label the ingredients in the whiskey because officials were suspicious that distillers were diluting the liquor by adding water, grain alcohol and prune juice to increase the quantity.

Drinking establishments went upscale, with speakeasies being converted into clubs where waiters wore black jackets and stiff white shirts. Membership lists were compiled to keep out the riffraff. Prohibition created a liquor shortage. Pittsburgh bars, hotels and restaurants were forced to continue selling bootleg whiskey and beer because of the limited legal supply, and the price for bonded whiskey was out of reach of most people during the Great Depression.

A case of bonded whiskey sold for $80.00 while the cheapest went for $38.00 a case. Pennsylvania charged the highest prices in the nation for bonded whiskey. A fifth of whiskey cost $6.50 while a quart sold for $8.00, compared to $3.00 and $4.25 for the same brands in Canada. Lawmakers were concerned that the high prices might rekindle the spread of speakeasies and start new gang wars between rival bootleggers.

Repeal didn't kill the speakeasy. Customers still patronized them because the drinks were cheaper—the owners didn't have to pay the state tax on booze. State tax agents quickly descended on bars and clubs in Pittsburgh and other large cities to ensure the places were licensed and the bottles had the required tax stamps. Agents also demanded to see bills of sale from the proprietors to make sure they were purchased legally.

Bootleggers opened two "wildcat breweries" in Pittsburgh after repeal, selling beer using forged labels of well-known breweries. To make the ersatz beer look like the real thing, they stole bottles and barrels from the Fort Pitt, Pittsburgh Brewing Company and the Independent Brewing Company.

Speakeasies remained a problem in Pittsburgh and western Pennsylvania. In the years following repeal, police continued to raid illegal drinking joints. In 1938, 125 places were raided. Federal agents raided 19 spots in the Hill District that same year. By 1975, speakeasies had proliferated in the Hill District, forcing Pittsburgh police and Liquor Control Enforcement agents to continue tracking illegal liquor. The LCE still conducts between twenty to thirty raids a year on speakeasies. In 2001, six men were shot in a Pittsburgh speakeasy, and another four were wounded in a 2005 shooting at a speakeasy in the city of New Kensington, north of Pittsburgh. Today, Pittsburgh has more bars per capita than any other city in the nation. There are twelve bars for every ten thousand residents in the city. The cost of a liquor license in Pittsburgh ranges from $75,000 to $80,000 while licenses in neighboring counties can run as high as $250,000.

11
Pinchot's Last Laugh

Gifford Pinchot's lasting legacy as governor has been the subject of legislative political battles since 1933 and continues to this day as Republicans and Democrats debate whether to privatize the state's chain of state liquor stores. Attempts to privatize the state stores have been met with resistance from public service unions and some politicians who support the labor movement. With repeal looming, Pinchot wanted to strictly control the sale of liquor and beer by having state-operated liquor stores in the hope that the inconvenience of purchasing liquor and its high cost would reduce drinking and rid the state of saloons forever. He also anticipated that high liquor taxes would generate enough money to fund relief programs during the Great Depression. Members of his own party were opposed to his plan, but Pinchot was ready to battle his fellow Republicans and threw down the political gauntlet. Saying, "Let politics go hang," he told the legislature in 1933, reported the *Pittsburgh Press*.

Pennsylvania found itself with twelve and a half million gallons of whiskey that had been stored in warehouses since 1920. Nicknamed "Sweepstakes" whiskey, it was not fully aged and contained extracts from wood chips to give the liquor color, although it was still 90 proof. Detractors called it "Pinchot Whiskey," which the governor ordered the state to sell for $1 a bottle in the hope of generating $575,000 in much-needed revenue.

Pittsburgh mayor William McNair, a Mennonite, opposed the sale of "Sweepstakes" whiskey and tried to start another whiskey rebellion by going to war with Pinchot. As mayor, McNair also sat as magistrate in Morals Court, hearing liquor-related cases. He dismissed some cases and refused to listen to testimony in others, allowing the defendants to get off. He dismissed a charge against a woman for having a bottle of untaxed whiskey in her possession, saying the only crime the woman was guilty of was "competing in the rotten liquor business with Governor Pinchot," reported the *Pittsburgh Press*.

When sixty drunks appeared before him on charges of public intoxication, McNair asked the men what they had been drinking. Each one blamed their stupor on "Pinchot Whiskey."

"How do you feel?" asked McNair, according to a story in the *Pittsburgh Press*.

"Rotten," they replied, to a man.

"What have you been drinking? Some of Pinchot's whiskey?"

"Yes, sir," they replied.

"Well, let's tell the governor about that," said McNair, who immediately called Pinchot's office in Harrisburg and talked to the governor's wife, Cornelia Bryce Pinchot. After talking with Mrs. Pinchot, McNair gave the telephone to one of the drunks.

"I tell you this is pretty bad stuff. I just took three drinks and I woke up in the police station," said the man.

McNair released all sixty men. After talking to McNair, Mrs. Pinchot told reporters that the drunk spoke "more coherently than Mr. McNair. I think that's sufficient comment, don't you?"

McNair tried to ban the sale of the cheap whiskey in Pittsburgh but was warned by state attorneys that he had no power to interfere with the operation of state stores. McNair, in a speech at the Pittsburgh YMCA, reported by the *Pittsburgh Press*, said he would lead the Woman's Christian Temperance Union in a bottle-smashing crusade against the city's state stores. He urged the young men in the audience to join him on a raid. He left the podium and marched to the lobby, followed by an aroused contingent, when he suddenly stopped.

"I was just joking," McNair said. "I have an appointment to play bridge."

McNair also blamed Pinchot for an increase in alcohol-related traffic deaths, reported the *Press*, charging the governor was allowing the sale of "Pinchot Whiskey," which he said was nothing more than "wood alcohol fixed up with a bit of coloring matter in our liquor stores."

Pinchot had his way. He pushed a tough liquor control law through the General Assembly that remains with Pennsylvania to this day. Pinchot imposed a one-dollar bottle tax on liquor made after Prohibition and a two-dollar bottle tax on liquor distilled prior to the ban.

As tensions mounted in the General Assembly between Pinchot and lawmakers, Pinchot stopped by the Senate Chambers in January 1933

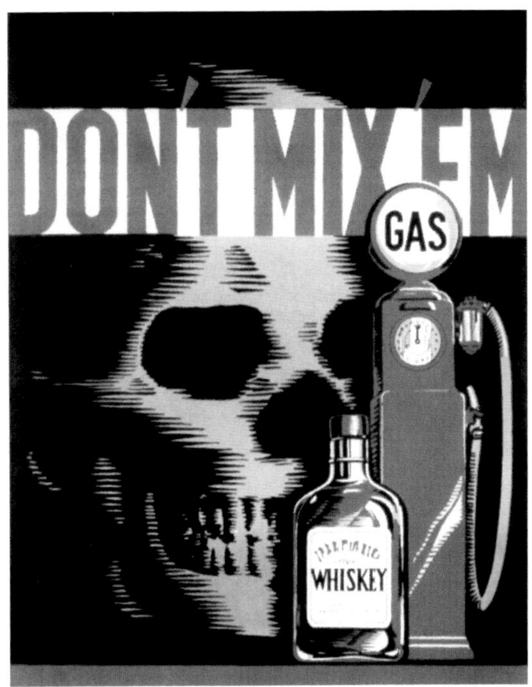

Pittsburgh mayor William McNair blamed Governor Pinchot for an increase in alcohol-related traffic deaths after the state began selling the cheap but potent "Sweepstakes Whiskey." *Library of Congress.*

to greet senators returning from the holiday break. One senator accused Pinchot of being a hypocrite because his wife reportedly was seen drinking at a party the day before. Pinchot was outraged and demanded the senator provide proof or apologize.

"I cannot horsewhip a senator, however much I desire to, and however much the senator deserves it," the *Pittsburgh Press* quoted Pinchot as saying.

Pinchot was a moralist who believed it was his duty as governor to regulate the behavior of Pennsylvania citizens. He was dismayed with repeal, believing liquor was "a moral wrong and an economic mistake. Prohibition at its worst has been infinitely better than booze at its best," reported the *Press*.

"Every Sunday the governor tries to make some changes in the universe where the Lord hasn't done it right," said state treasurer Charles Snyder in the *Pittsburgh Press*.

On November 13, 1933, Pinchot's plan was presented to the General Assembly, and nine days later, the House approved his measure by a vote of 144 to 61. On November 28, the Senate approved it by a vote of 33 to 14. The bill was amended and re-amended a number of times before final passage. One senator argued the state store system would put Pennsylvania

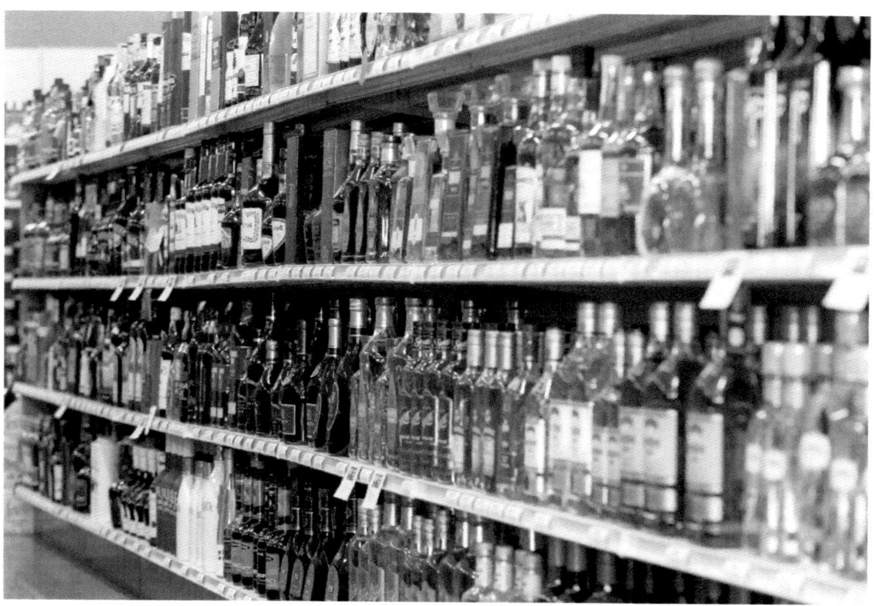

Shelves of liquor at a Pennsylvania State Store. *Library of Congress.*

in the red. Another mistakenly predicted that the bill was "born in politics, raised in politics and will die in politics."

The first state stores opened on January 2, 1934. They've remained in state hands ever since. More than six hundred stores generate more than $2.3 billion a year in revenue, according to the Pennsylvania Liquor Control Board.

"I congratulate you upon an unprecedented achievement," Pinchot told lawmakers. "You have adopted the best system of liquor control yet devised in America."

Bibliography

Abrams, Robert I. "Alcohol, Drugs and the National Pastime." *Journal of Labor and Employment Law* 8, no. 4 (2006): 861–82.

Address of Governor Franklin D. Roosevelt, October 19, 1932. Forbes Field, Pittsburgh, Pennsylvania. fdrlibrary.marist,edu.

Afro-American. "Broke Leg, Turns Bootlegger." September 4, 1926.

Allen, Frederick Lewis. *Only Yesterday. An Informal History of the 1920s*. New York: Open Road.

Andren, Kari. "Pennsylvania Liquor Licenses Are Considered 'Better Than Gold.'" *Greensburg Tribune-Review*, July 20, 2014.

Andren, Kari, and Paul Pierce. "Alcohol Law Still Pursuing Speakeasy Operators." *Greensburg Tribune-Review*, November 1, 2014.

Astorino, Samuel J. "The Contested Senate Election of William Scott Vare." *Pennsylvania History*, no. 2 (April 1961): 187–201.

Baldwin, Leland. *Pittsburgh: The Story of a City, 1750–1865*. Pittsburgh: University of Pittsburgh Press.

———. *Whiskey Rebels: The Story of a Frontier Uprising*. Pittsburgh: University of Pittsburgh Press, 1939.

Batz, Bob. "Craft Distilleries Are Opening Across the Region, Creating Good Libations (and Expectations)." *Pittsburgh Post-Gazette*, August 9, 2015.

Baubie, James. "Traffic County by Boy Scouts Reveals What a Great Problem Pittsburgh Faces." *Pittsburgh Press*, December 1, 1929.

Bauman, John, and Edward K. Muller. *Before Renaissance. Planning in Pittsburgh, 1889–1947*. Pittsburgh: University of Pittsburgh Press, 2011.

Beers, Paul. *Pennsylvania Politics Today and Yesterday*. University Park: Pennsylvania State University Press, 1980.

Behr, Edward. *Prohibition. Thirteen Years That Changed America*. New York: Arcade Publishing, 1996.

Black, Conrad. *Franklin Delano Roosevelt. Champion of Freedom*. New York: Public Affairs, 2003.

Blum, Deborah. *The Poisoner's Handbook: Murder and the Birth of Forensic Medicine in Jazz Age New York*. New York: Penguin Press, 2010.

Blumenthal, Karen. *Bootleg: Murder, Moonshine, and the Lawless Years of Prohibition*. New York: Roaring Book Press, 2011.

Boucher, John Newton, and John W. Jordan. *A Century and a Half of Pittsburgh and Her People*. Vol. 1. New York: Lewis Publishing Co., 1908.

Brewer, John M., Jr. *Pittsburgh Jazz*. Charleston, SC: Arcadia Publishing, 2007.

Bunie, Andrew. *Robert L. Vann of the Pittsburgh Courier: Politics and Black Journalism*. Pittsburgh: University of Pittsburgh Press, 1974.

Burgess, Ellis Beaver. *History of the Pittsburgh Synod of the General Synod of the Evangelical Lutheran Church*. Philadelphia: Lutheran Publication Society, 1904.

Burns, Eric. *The Spirits of America: A Social History of Alcohol*. Philadelphia: Temple University Press, 2004.

Byington, Margaret F. *The Pittsburgh Survey*. Vol. 4, *Homestead: The Household of Mill Towns*. New York: Charities Publication Commission, 1910.

Campbell, Maurice. "Campbell Begins Dry Law Expose." *Pittsburgh Press*, November 5, 1930.

———. "Official Tells of Orders Sent from Treasury." *Pittsburgh Press*, October 8, 1930.

Canadine, David. *Andrew Mellon: An American Life*. New York: Vintage Books, 2008.

Church, Samuel Harden. "The Paradise of the Ostrich." *North American Review*, Summer 1925, 625–30.

Clarke, Paul. "The Comeback Kid: Rye Whiskey." *Imbibe* magazine, January 20, 2009.

Coates, Bob. "Troopers Aid in Search for Killer of Pal." *Pittsburgh Press*, August 1, 1929.

Cohen, Jeannie. "Drink Some Whiskey and Call in the Morning." History.com, January 17, 2002.

Comte, Julien. "The Next Page: The Lessons of Prohibition." *Pittsburgh Post-Gazette*, February 3, 2008.

Dorsett, Lyle. *Billy Sunday and the Redemption of Urban America*. Macon, GA: Mercer University Press, 2004.

Dressler, C.W. "Pinchot Gets Liquor Store's Bill." *Pittsburgh Post-Gazette*, November 29, 1933.

Duffus, R.L. "Is Pittsburgh Civilized?" *Harper's Monthly* 161 (October 1930).

English, T.J. *Havana Nocturne: How the Mob Owned Cuba—Then Lost It in the Revolution*. New York: Harper, 2008.

Gage, Beverly. "Just What the Doctor Ordered." *Smithsonian Magazine*, April 2005.

Gazette Times. "Charges Are Made Against Saloonists." March 12, 1914.

———. "Council Fires Chief, 9 Cops; Young Captain Sole Survivor." December 17, 1926.

———. "Drive on Beer Camps Opened." August 1, 1924.

———. "Dry Agents Swoop Down on 22 Eagle Lodges Here." December 24, 1926.

———. "Insane Slayer Escapes from County Home." November 28, 1915.

———. "Legal Liquor Rackets Hit in Dry Report." July 20, 1935.

———. "Liquor Seized in Raid On Undertaking Rooms." December 20, 1919.

———. "Mark Five More for Deaths in Wilmerding." December 15, 1926.

———. "One Slain as Beer War Breaks." July 5, 1933.

———. "Police Describe Three Who Shot Volpe Brothers," July 30, 1932.

———. "Police Guarding Herron's Home." June 3, 1933.

———. "Pittsburgh 'Sherlock' Follows Nose in Hunt for Dry Law Breakers." November 6, 1919.

———. "Prohibition Is Biggest Swindle in Our History." July 4, 1927.

———. "Railroads Loose $25,000,000 Yearly in Thefts from Cars, Chief W.J. Flynn Says Here." May 31, 1919.

———. "Urge Gardner to Wipe Out Terrorism in Wilmerding." December 23, 1926.

———. "Whiskey Thieves Active; 2,500 Guards Wanted." January 15, 1920.

———. "Wilmerding One of Cleanest in County, Gardner Says." December 17, 1926.

George, James R. "Celebrator 'Crossed Up' Declares Record 'Ruint.'" *Pittsburgh Post-Gazette*, December 4, 1933.

Greenberg, Martin Alan. *Citizens Defending America from Colonial Times to the Age of Terrorism*. Pittsburgh: University of Pittsburgh Press, 2005.

Heineman, Kenneth J. *A Catholic New Deal: Religion and Reform in Depression Pittsburgh*. University Park: Pennsylvania State University Press, 1989.

Henle, Raymond. "Dr. Church Urges New Party Formed to Fight Dry Law." *Pittsburgh Post-Gazette*, February 21, 1930.

Henry Clay Frick Business Records. Boxes 2 and 3, Archives of Industrial Society, University of Pittsburgh.

Hinshaw, John. *Steelworkers. Race and Class Struggle in Twentieth-Century Pittsburgh*. Albany: State University of New York Press, 2012.

History of the Woman's Christian Temperance Union Crusade and Allegheny County Woman's Christian Temperance Union. Box 3, Archives of Industrial Society, University of Pittsburgh.

Hogeland, William. *The Whiskey Rebellion*. New York: Scribner, 2006.

Hoover, Herbert. *The Memoirs of Herbert Hoover: The Great Depression, 1929–1941*. New York: Macmillan, 1952.

Hunt, Thomas, and Michael A. Tona. "A Test of Resolve: The 1932 Murder of Pittsburgh Mafia Boss John Bazzano." *Informer: The History of American Crime and Law Enforcement*, January 2011.

Johnson, Charles P. "Before Revolutionary War, Speakeasies Existed, Called Tippling Houses." *Pittsburgh Press*, August 23, 1932.

Johnson, Robert. "City Police Track Down Illegal Booze." *Pittsburgh Press*, August 31, 1975.

Kleinberg, S.J. *The Shadow of the Mills: Working-Class Families in Pittsburgh, 1870–1907*. Pittsburgh: University of Pittsburgh Press, 1989.

Kobler, John. *Ardent Spirts: The Rise and Fall of Prohibition*. New York: De Capo Press, 1993.

Kraut, Alan M. *The Huddled Masses: The Immigrants in American Society, 1880–1921*. Wheeling, IL: Harlan-Davidson Inc., 1982.

Kyving, David E., *Daily Life in the United States, 1920–1940. How Americans Lived Through the Roaring Twenties and the Great Depression*. Chicago: Ivan R. Dee, 2002.

Lender, Mark Edward, and James Kirby Martin. *Drinking in America: A History*. New York: Free Press, 1982.

Literary Digest. "States Preparing for the Great Repeal Battle." March 4, 1933.

Literary Guild. "How Wet Is Pennsylvania?" November 10, 1923.

Lorant, Stefan. *Pittsburgh: The Story of an American City*. 5th ed. Pittsburgh: Esselmont Books LLC, 1999.

Love, Philip H. *Andrew W. Mellon: The Man and His Work*. Baltimore, MD: Coggens & Company, 1929.

Martinelli, Patricia A. *True Pennsylvania Crime: The State's Most Notorious Criminal Cases*. Mechanicsburg, PA: Stackpole Books, 2008.

McDevitt, Bette. "The William Penn Speakeasy." *Western Pennsylvania History*, Fall 2014.

McFarland, Kermit. "Pinchot Made Goat in State Liquor Probe." *Pittsburgh Press*, February 28, 1935.

McGirr, Lisa. *The War on Alcohol: Prohibition and the Rise of the American State.* New York: W.W. Norton & Company, 2015.

Mellon, Steve. "Pittsburgh: The Dark Years." *Pittsburgh Post-Gazette*, April 14, 2014.

Milligan, Alice. "The Club's the Thing." *Pittsburgh Press*, November 11, 1934.

Newton, Michael. *Mr. Mob: The Life and Crimes of Moe Dalitz.* Jefferson, NC: McFarland, 2007.

New York Times. "Demons Loose in New Orleans." March 15, 1891.

———. "The Illegal Speakeasy; Defiance of the Law in Pennsylvania." July 6, 1891.

Okrent, Daniel. *Last Call: The Rise and Fall of Prohibition.* New York: Scribner, 2010.

Osborn, Matthew Warner. *Rum Maniacs: Alcoholic Insanity in the Early American Republic.* Chicago: University of Chicago Press, 2014.

Panunzio, Constantine. "The Foreign Born and Prohibition." *Annals of the American Academy of Political and Social Science*, 1932.

Peck, Garrett, *Prohibition in Washington, D.C.: How Dry We Weren't.* Charleston, SC: The History Press, 2011.

Persico, Joseph. "Vendetta in New Orleans." *American Heritage* 24, no. 4 (June 1973). americanheritage.com/users/joseph-e-persico.

Philadelphia Evening Ledger. "Federal Probe in Booze Bribery." December 6, 1922.

Pilgrim, Robert J. *The Strip: A Socio-Religious Survey of a Typical Problem of Pittsburgh.* Pittsburgh: Christian Social Services Union, 1915.

Pittsburgh Brewing Company Scrapbooks, 1907–1911. Box 1, Archives of Industrial Society, University of Pittsburgh.

Pittsburgh Chronicle-Telegram. "Would Shut Off Slavs' Drinks." September 27, 1907.

Pittsburgh Courier. "Close Dives in Hill District, Police, Federal Officers Urged." December 12, 1925.

———. "Dry Agent, Walking with Wife, Attacked." December 12, 1925.

———. "Rev. Hightower Leads Raids on Vice in Hill." March 31, 1928.

Pittsburgh Oral Histories. MW by Barry Chad, January 21, 2007. Carnegie Library of Pittsburgh.

Pittsburgh Post-Gazette. "Appeal Argued for Tom Coyne." September 25, 1934.

———. "Arrests Stir Gang Turmoil." May 5, 1933.

———. "Beer Truck Hits Auto; Four Hurt." December 4, 1933.

———. "Big Bootleg Profit Told by Roxie Long." December 1, 1932.

———. "Bombing in City Grows." May 31, 1933.

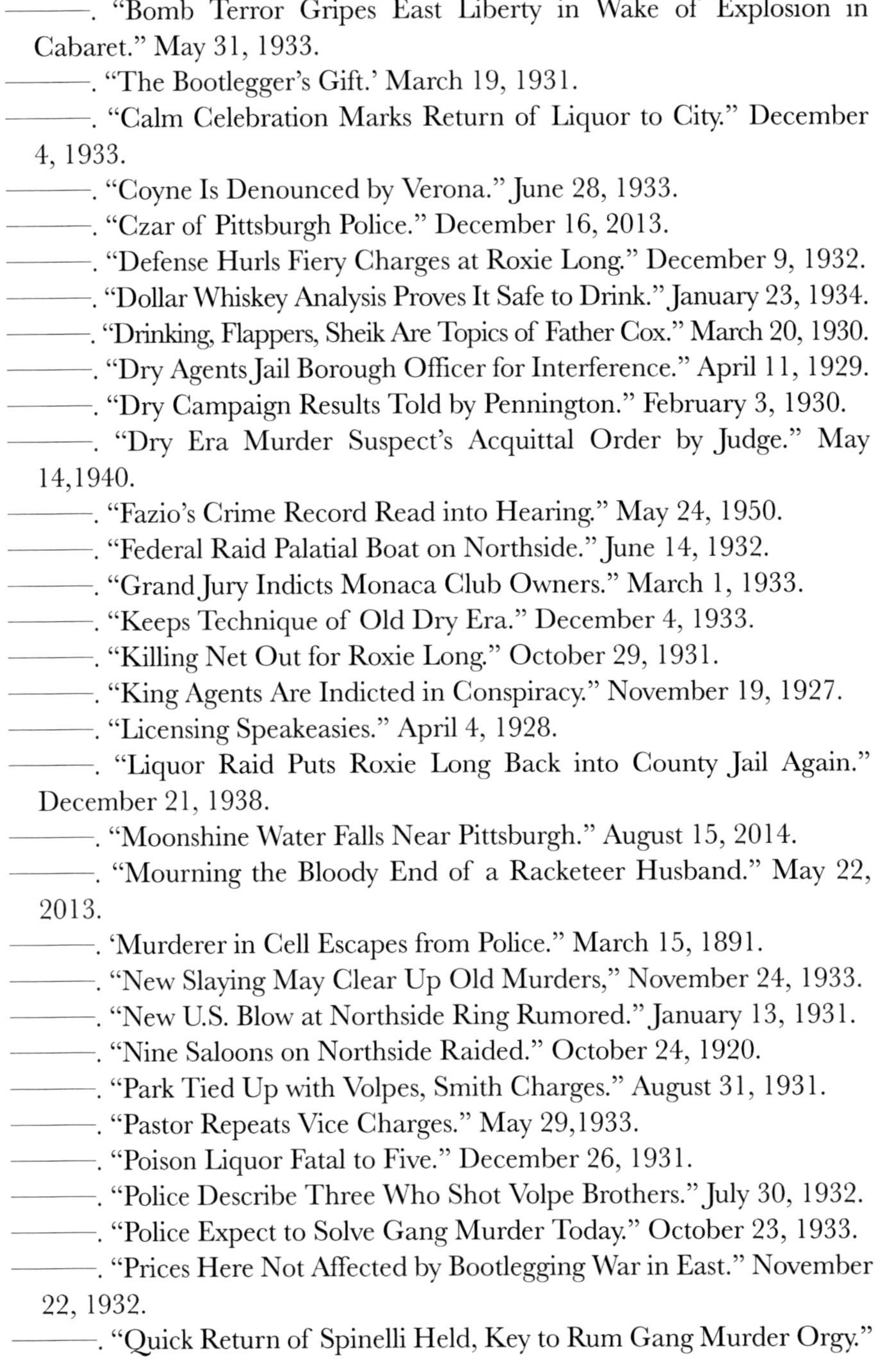

———. "Bomb Terror Gripes East Liberty in Wake of Explosion in Cabaret." May 31, 1933.
———. "The Bootlegger's Gift.' March 19, 1931.
———. "Calm Celebration Marks Return of Liquor to City." December 4, 1933.
———. "Coyne Is Denounced by Verona." June 28, 1933.
———. "Czar of Pittsburgh Police." December 16, 2013.
———. "Defense Hurls Fiery Charges at Roxie Long." December 9, 1932.
———. "Dollar Whiskey Analysis Proves It Safe to Drink." January 23, 1934.
———. "Drinking, Flappers, Sheik Are Topics of Father Cox." March 20, 1930.
———. "Dry Agents Jail Borough Officer for Interference." April 11, 1929.
———. "Dry Campaign Results Told by Pennington." February 3, 1930.
———. "Dry Era Murder Suspect's Acquittal Order by Judge." May 14,1940.
———. "Fazio's Crime Record Read into Hearing." May 24, 1950.
———. "Federal Raid Palatial Boat on Northside." June 14, 1932.
———. "Grand Jury Indicts Monaca Club Owners." March 1, 1933.
———. "Keeps Technique of Old Dry Era." December 4, 1933.
———. "Killing Net Out for Roxie Long." October 29, 1931.
———. "King Agents Are Indicted in Conspiracy." November 19, 1927.
———. "Licensing Speakeasies." April 4, 1928.
———. "Liquor Raid Puts Roxie Long Back into County Jail Again." December 21, 1938.
———. "Moonshine Water Falls Near Pittsburgh." August 15, 2014.
———. "Mourning the Bloody End of a Racketeer Husband." May 22, 2013.
———. 'Murderer in Cell Escapes from Police." March 15, 1891.
———. "New Slaying May Clear Up Old Murders," November 24, 1933.
———. "New U.S. Blow at Northside Ring Rumored." January 13, 1931.
———. "Nine Saloons on Northside Raided." October 24, 1920.
———. "Park Tied Up with Volpes, Smith Charges." August 31, 1931.
———. "Pastor Repeats Vice Charges." May 29,1933.
———. "Poison Liquor Fatal to Five." December 26, 1931.
———. "Police Describe Three Who Shot Volpe Brothers." July 30, 1932.
———. "Police Expect to Solve Gang Murder Today." October 23, 1933.
———. "Prices Here Not Affected by Bootlegging War in East." November 22, 1932.
———. "Quick Return of Spinelli Held, Key to Rum Gang Murder Orgy." October 25, 1933.

———. "Racket King Is Slain in Northside." August 7, 1929.
———. "Rackets Permitted to Resume to Help Finance Fall Campaign." May 29, 1933.
———. "Release Man Held in Killing." August 5, 1929.
———. "Repeal Proclamation Issued by President." December 4, 1933.
———. "Rivals Strangle Rum Racket Chief with Own Necktie." March 19, 1930.
———. "Roxie Long Gives Up On Himself." April 18, 1959.
———. "Roxie's 'Home' Raided Again." January 11, 1933.
———. "Strike-Break Heads Blamed for Vice Reign." January 24, 1928.
———. "Stubenrach Back Again on Police Force." April 9, 1931.
———. "Terrorism in a Borough." April 13, 1929.
———. "Thousands Attend Funeral of Slain Gangster Chief." August 12, 1929.
———. "Throngs Jam Clubs and Restaurants to Hail Return of Legal Liquor." December 4, 1933.
———. "Volpes Buried Brother with Huge Funeral." July 30, 1932.
———. "Water Under the Bridge." August 14, 1957.
———. "Whatever Happened to Santo Bazzano," December 6, 2013.
———. "Wine Delivery Interrupted." December 6, 1929.
Pittsburgh Press. "Alcohol Seizure Upheld by Court." February 18, 1927.
———. "'Big Gorilla' Soars to Racket Heights, Takes Tribute Until Bullets Stop Him." July 31, 1932.
———. "Bootleg Beer Being Distributed with Fake Labels." June 14, 1933.
———. "Bootleg Clan Here Glum as Repeal Nears." November 9, 1933.
———. "Bootleggers Laugh as Dry Navy Strikes at 'Base of Liquor Supply' Off New England Coast." May 27, 1925.
———. "Bootlegging Crops Up in Liquor Here." December 14, 1942.
———. "Booze Ban Stands." December 8, 1919.
———. "Booze Raid on Northside." January 5, 1920.
———. "Checks Give Clue to Slaying of Four." October 6, 1930.
———. "City Is Divided on Dry Birthday." January 6, 1930.
———. "Claim Coal Police Block Probe." January 23, 1928.
———. "Cleanup Starts." April 18, 1933.
———. "Court Jam Aids Bootleggers." January 13, 1930.
———. "Crazed with Drink, Man Attacks Woman Before Ending Life." October 7, 1919.
———. "Crime and Repeal." April 14, 1934.
———. "Crime Wave Here Unchecked." February 5, 1919.

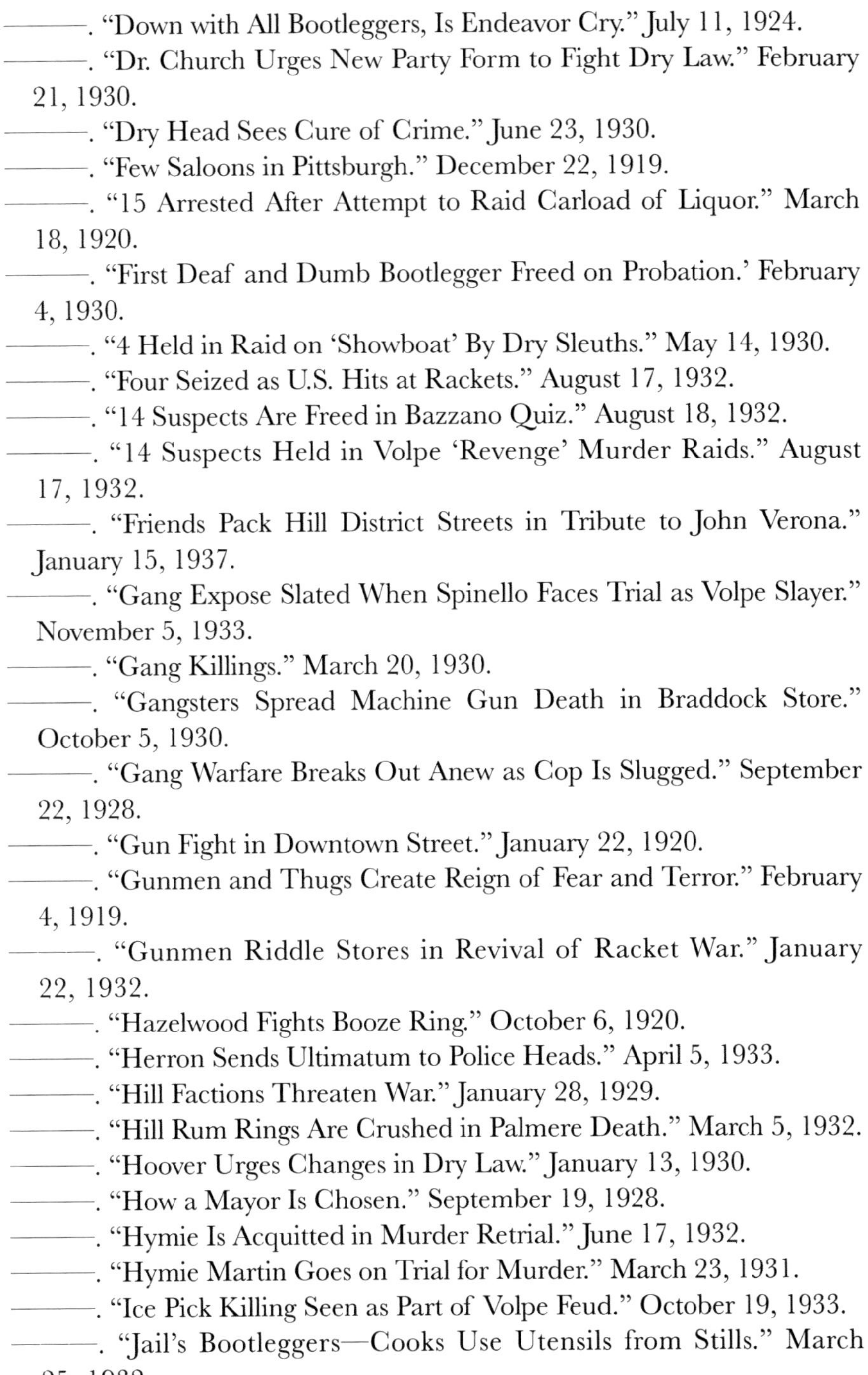

———. “Down with All Bootleggers, Is Endeavor Cry.” July 11, 1924.
———. “Dr. Church Urges New Party Form to Fight Dry Law.” February 21, 1930.
———. “Dry Head Sees Cure of Crime.” June 23, 1930.
———. “Few Saloons in Pittsburgh.” December 22, 1919.
———. “15 Arrested After Attempt to Raid Carload of Liquor.” March 18, 1920.
———. “First Deaf and Dumb Bootlegger Freed on Probation.’ February 4, 1930.
———. “4 Held in Raid on ‘Showboat’ By Dry Sleuths.” May 14, 1930.
———. “Four Seized as U.S. Hits at Rackets.” August 17, 1932.
———. “14 Suspects Are Freed in Bazzano Quiz.” August 18, 1932.
———. “14 Suspects Held in Volpe ‘Revenge’ Murder Raids.” August 17, 1932.
———. “Friends Pack Hill District Streets in Tribute to John Verona.” January 15, 1937.
———. “Gang Expose Slated When Spinello Faces Trial as Volpe Slayer.” November 5, 1933.
———. “Gang Killings.” March 20, 1930.
———. “Gangsters Spread Machine Gun Death in Braddock Store.” October 5, 1930.
———. “Gang Warfare Breaks Out Anew as Cop Is Slugged.” September 22, 1928.
———. “Gun Fight in Downtown Street.” January 22, 1920.
———. “Gunmen and Thugs Create Reign of Fear and Terror.” February 4, 1919.
———. “Gunmen Riddle Stores in Revival of Racket War.” January 22, 1932.
———. “Hazelwood Fights Booze Ring.” October 6, 1920.
———. “Herron Sends Ultimatum to Police Heads.” April 5, 1933.
———. “Hill Factions Threaten War.” January 28, 1929.
———. “Hill Rum Rings Are Crushed in Palmere Death.” March 5, 1932.
———. “Hoover Urges Changes in Dry Law.” January 13, 1930.
———. “How a Mayor Is Chosen.” September 19, 1928.
———. “Hymie Is Acquitted in Murder Retrial.” June 17, 1932.
———. “Hymie Martin Goes on Trial for Murder.” March 23, 1931.
———. “Ice Pick Killing Seen as Part of Volpe Feud.” October 19, 1933.
———. “Jail’s Bootleggers—Cooks Use Utensils from Stills.” March 25, 1932.

———. "Joe 'the Ghost' Most Hated of Gangsters Here, Gives Enemies Lessons in Dodging Bullets." August 4, 1932.
———. "Judge Orders Vice Cleanup." September 5, 1932.
———. "Jury Examines Bank Accounts in Liquor Quiz." September 10, 1928.
———. "Jury Gets Appeal of Volpe Brothers." November 19, 1930.
———. "Liggett Brands Vice of City Worst in Land." July 10, 1930.
———. "Liquor Hard to Get, Even at Profiteer Prices Here." December 5, 1933.
———. "Liquor Prices Peril State Revenue." December 26, 1933.
———. "Liquor Ring Workings Bared." October 31, 1928.
———. "Louis Volpe, Two Others Seized in Raid." May 4, 1933.
———. "McNair Blames Pinchot in Gain in Traffic Deaths." March 28, 1934.
———. "Mellon to Lose Dry Law Power." January 13, 1930.
———. "Ministers Hot in Denouncing Booze Cheats." October 6, 1920.
———. "Ministers Urge Prosecution of Booze Charges." October 6, 1924.
———. "Monastero's Gang of Racketeers Got Its Start by Hi-Jacking; Foes' Guns End their Reign," Aug. 1, 1932.
———. "Much Sought 'Al' Capone 'Drops In' On McKees Rocks." March 21, 1930.
———. "Mysterious Bazzano's Life Unlike Volpes; but Greed Leads All 4 to Gangster Deaths." August 12, 1932.
———. "New Beer's Eve Lid Clamped On." April 5, 1933.
———. "New Gambling House Exposed by Patterson." September 15, 1932.
———. "No Decision on Beer," December 22, 1919.
———. "Padlock Faced by Monaca Club." January 29, 1933.
———. "Patterson Demands Cleanup of Vice; Denounces Protection Given Resort." September 5, 1932.
———. "Pennsylvania Ratifies Repeal." December 5, 1933.
———. "Pinchot Hits Mellon on Dry Law." July 5, 1925.
———. "Pinchot Planning to Close Saloons in Pittsburgh." October 12, 1923.
———. "Pittsburgh Big Source of Beer Is Testimony." February 5, 1925.
———. "Pittsburgh's 'Death Kill' Girl Jailed in Gang Killing." October 22, 1933.
———. "Pittsburgh Women Voice Repeal Sentiment in New Style." February 10, 1933.
———. "Police, Coroner Clash in Volpe Probe." September 23, 1932.
———. "Preachers on Prohibition." August 20, 1928.

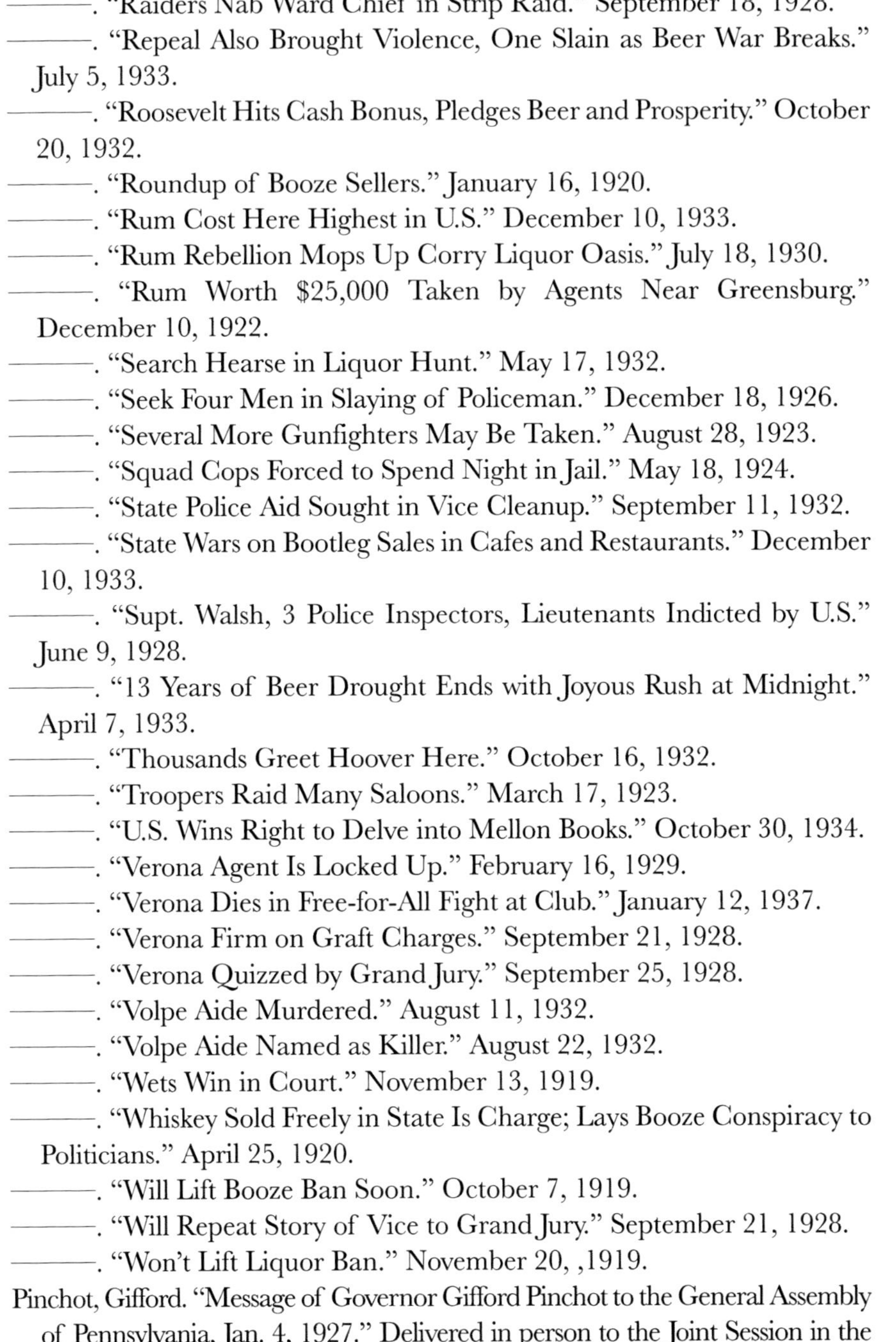

———. "Raiders Nab Ward Chief in Strip Raid." September 18, 1928.
———. "Repeal Also Brought Violence, One Slain as Beer War Breaks." July 5, 1933.
———. "Roosevelt Hits Cash Bonus, Pledges Beer and Prosperity." October 20, 1932.
———. "Roundup of Booze Sellers." January 16, 1920.
———. "Rum Cost Here Highest in U.S." December 10, 1933.
———. "Rum Rebellion Mops Up Corry Liquor Oasis." July 18, 1930.
———. "Rum Worth $25,000 Taken by Agents Near Greensburg." December 10, 1922.
———. "Search Hearse in Liquor Hunt." May 17, 1932.
———. "Seek Four Men in Slaying of Policeman." December 18, 1926.
———. "Several More Gunfighters May Be Taken." August 28, 1923.
———. "Squad Cops Forced to Spend Night in Jail." May 18, 1924.
———. "State Police Aid Sought in Vice Cleanup." September 11, 1932.
———. "State Wars on Bootleg Sales in Cafes and Restaurants." December 10, 1933.
———. "Supt. Walsh, 3 Police Inspectors, Lieutenants Indicted by U.S." June 9, 1928.
———. "13 Years of Beer Drought Ends with Joyous Rush at Midnight." April 7, 1933.
———. "Thousands Greet Hoover Here." October 16, 1932.
———. "Troopers Raid Many Saloons." March 17, 1923.
———. "U.S. Wins Right to Delve into Mellon Books." October 30, 1934.
———. "Verona Agent Is Locked Up." February 16, 1929.
———. "Verona Dies in Free-for-All Fight at Club." January 12, 1937.
———. "Verona Firm on Graft Charges." September 21, 1928.
———. "Verona Quizzed by Grand Jury." September 25, 1928.
———. "Volpe Aide Murdered." August 11, 1932.
———. "Volpe Aide Named as Killer." August 22, 1932.
———. "Wets Win in Court." November 13, 1919.
———. "Whiskey Sold Freely in State Is Charge; Lays Booze Conspiracy to Politicians." April 25, 1920.
———. "Will Lift Booze Ban Soon." October 7, 1919.
———. "Will Repeat Story of Vice to Grand Jury." September 21, 1928.
———. "Won't Lift Liquor Ban." November 20, ,1919.
Pinchot, Gifford. "Message of Governor Gifford Pinchot to the General Assembly of Pennsylvania, Jan. 4, 1927." Delivered in person to the Joint Session in the House of Representatives, January 4, 1927, Harrisburg, Pennsylvania.

Pitz, Marylynne. "1920 to 1939: From Speakeasies to Harlem Nights." *Pittsburgh Post-Gazette*, April 18, 2004.

Rimmel, William. "Ghosts of Lurid Past Tread Hill Rubble." *Pittsburgh Post-Gazette*, June 18, 1956.

———. "Law Can't See Gambling." *Pittsburgh Post-Gazette*, August 25, 1958.

Roddan, Edward L. "Vice Orgy Bared in Pennsylvania Primary," Milwaukee Sentinel, June 17, 1926.

Shlaes, Amity. *The Forgotten Man. A New History of the Great Depression*. New York: Harper Perennial, 2008.

Simonich, Milan. "Shootings a Reminder Speakeasies Still Exist." *Pittsburgh Post-Gazette*, February 18, 2005.

Skrabec, Quentin R., Jr. *Henry Clay Frick: The Life of the Perfect Capitalist*. Jefferson, NC: McFarland, 2010.

Sponholtz, Lloyd L. "Pittsburgh and Temperance, 1830–1854." *Western Pennsylvania History Magazine*, no. 4 (October 1963): 4–27.

Sprigle, Ray. "The Chinless Wonder." *Pittsburgh Post-Gazette*, October 30, 1949.

Stewart, Eliza Daniel, *Memories of the Great Crusade: A Thrilling Account of the Great Uprising of the Women of Ohio in 1873, Against the Liquor Crime*. Chicago: H.J. Smith Company, 1890.

The Strip: A Socio-Religious Survey of a Typical Problem Section of Pittsburgh, Pa. Pittsburgh: Christian Social Service Union, 1915.

"A Summary of Facts and Figures Dealing with Prohibition." Cincinnati: Wholesale Liquor Dealers Association, 1918.

Taylor, Robert. "Bulk of Liquor Seized in District Comes from Small Bootleggers, Figures Reveal." *Pittsburgh Press*, July 7, 1932.

———. "Prohibition Law Doubles Federal Court Expenses." *Pittsburgh Press*, July 8, 1932.

Thomas, Clarke. *Front-Page Pittsburgh: Two Hundred Years of the* Post-Gazette. Pittsburgh: University of Pittsburgh Press, 2005.

Toland, Bill. "Prohibition Ended 80 Years Ago Today, but the Dry Movement Never Worked Here." *Pittsburgh Post-Gazette*, December 4, 2013.

Townley, John B. "Racket Charges Fly in Hill Flare-Up." *Pittsburgh Press*, September 10, 1930.

Turzillo, Jane Ann. *Wicked Women of Northeast Ohio*. Charleston, SC: The History Press, 2011.

Watson, Kenneth. "Congressmen of District Divided on Dry Plan." *Pittsburgh Press*, January 6, 1930.

West, Allie. "How Pittsburgh Is Becoming a Beer and Spirts Destination." *Saveur*, January 7, 2016.

Whelan, Frank. "An Answer to the End of Prohibition: State Liquor Stores Are Legacy of Former Pa. Gov. Gifford Pinchot." *Morning Call*, February 23, 1997.

Van Atta, Robert. "Repeal of Prohibition Brought End to 14 Years of Law Enforcement Stories." *Greensburg Tribune-Review*, April 6, 2001.

Willard, Frances E. *Glimpse of Fifty Years: The Autobiography of an American Woman*. Chicago: H.J. Smith & Co., 1889.

Zahniser, Keith A. *Steel City Gospel: Protestant Laity and Reform in Progressive Era Pittsburgh*. New York: Routledge, 2005.

Index

About the Author

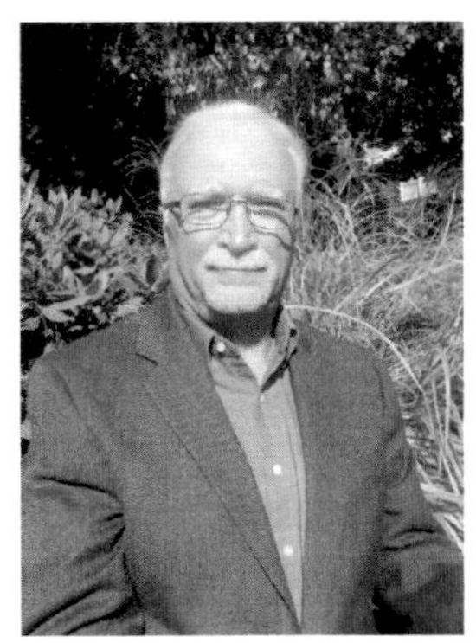

Richard Gazarik has been a journalist in western Pennsylvania for more than forty years. He is the author of *Black Valley: The Life and Death of Fannie Sellins* published in 2011.